Art Studio Feast

Broken things can be beautiful things

Early childhood explorations in play and art

MARTA CABRAL

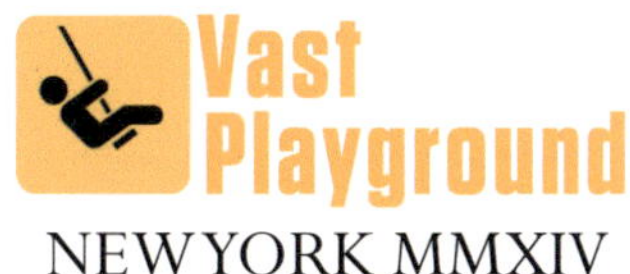

NEW YORK MMXIV

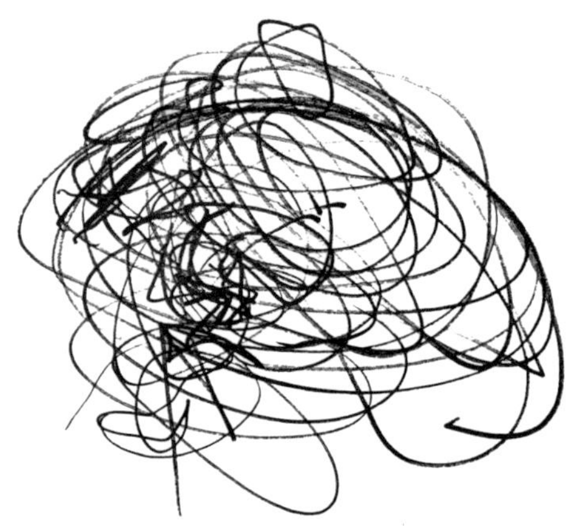

Author contact email: marta@martacabral.com

Published by
Vast Playground
1732 1st Ave., # 21515
New York, NY 10128

Interior photographs courtesy of Marta Cabral, Jono Rotman, Tran Templeton and Albert Whangbo.
Book design by Dennis Stevens.

ISBN 978-1-941796-00-9

Printed in the United States of America

"Here is where poetry showed up, at this intersection of a glimmer of self-knowledge and the need to make art of whatever materials are at hand."

- Joy Harjo

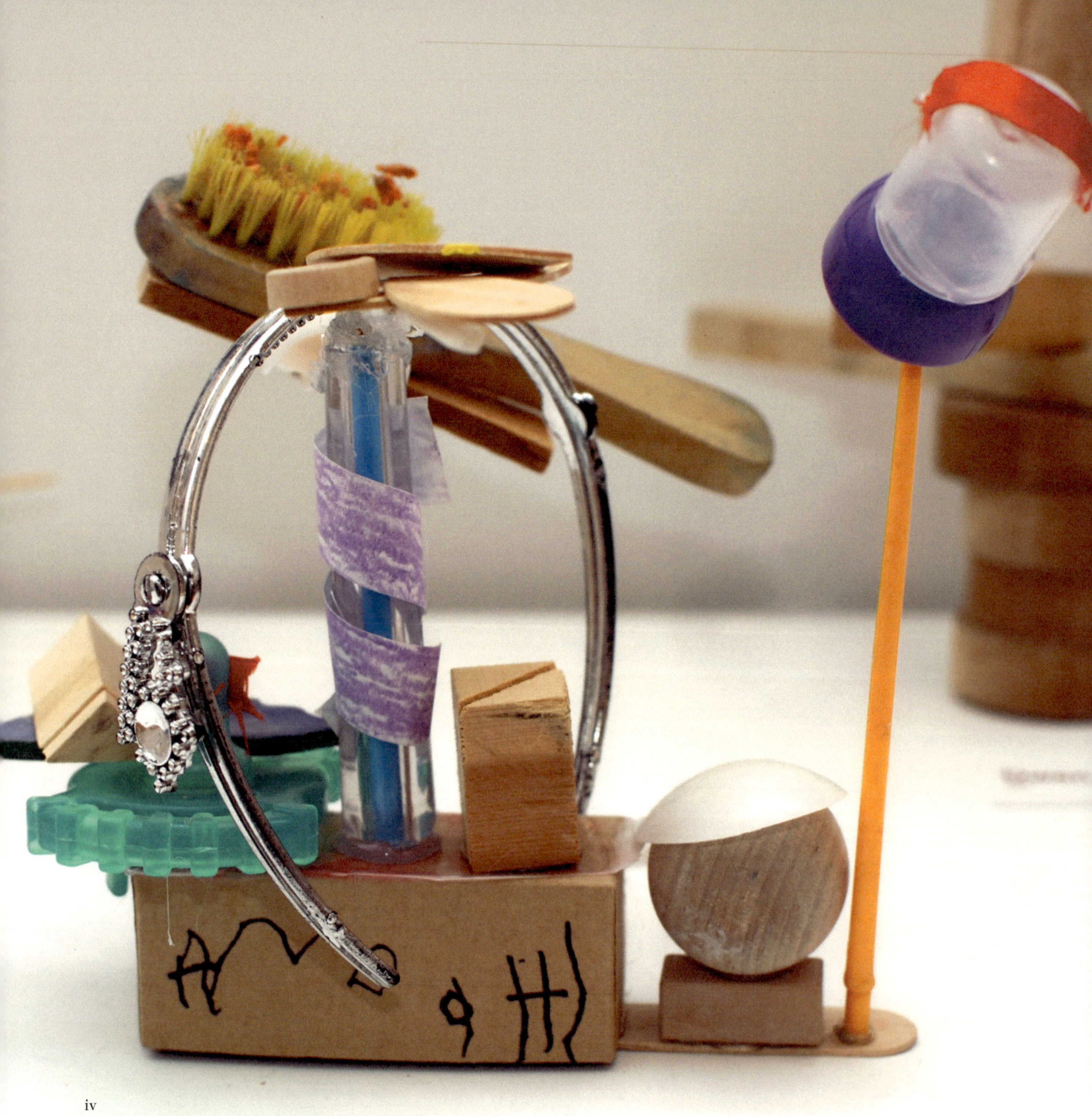

TABLE OF CONTENTS

FOREWORD

by Judith Burton
Professor and Faculty Director
Program of Art and Art Education
Teachers College, Columbia University

Speaking on behalf of my colleagues in the Art and Art Education Program here at Teachers College, the exhibition of work made by the young people of the Rita Gold Center has become one of the highlights of our Macy Art Gallery schedule.

The works of these young artists enliven us all with their freshness, spontaneity, and imagination. They also remind us that artmaking contributes to serious learning about the many and different ways in which materials such as paint, crayon, wood, and clay become voices through and in which to construct important ideas, observations, experiences, and meanings.

In this sense the Rita Gold community demonstrates that all children have the innate capacity to "speak through their art." We are also reminded each year that one of the greatest accomplishments of human culture, the creation of art, begins here deeply rooted in the exploratory activities of infants, toddlers, and young children. To be present each year to these moments of birth and emergence is moving and breathtaking.

Of course none of this extraordinary and important learning will take place without the right kinds of supports from the adult world. The Rita Gold Center offers a pedagogical environment in which grown-ups enter into exploration and learning with children, listening and dialoguing with them, encouraging them to develop, and own their thoughts as they find expression in the materials of art.

Artmaking is folded into the everyday world of the Rita Gold children, which makes it a crossroad experience that draws upon and integrates many different ways of knowing and presenting knowledge in visual forms. One of the unique features of the Center, of course, is the opportunity the children have to become frequent Macy Art Gallery visitors.

It has become an almost everyday (and delightful) occurrence for us to encounter groups of children in the Gallery thoughtfully paying attention to, or questioning, the work on the walls or the sculptures freestanding in the Gallery. Indeed, art teacher Marta Cabral is making a very unique contribution to the education of young children through the curatorial and critiquing work she carries out and is now writing about.

Once again, I thank the children and the teachers of Rita Gold for sharing yourselves so richly and lovingly with the Teachers College community.

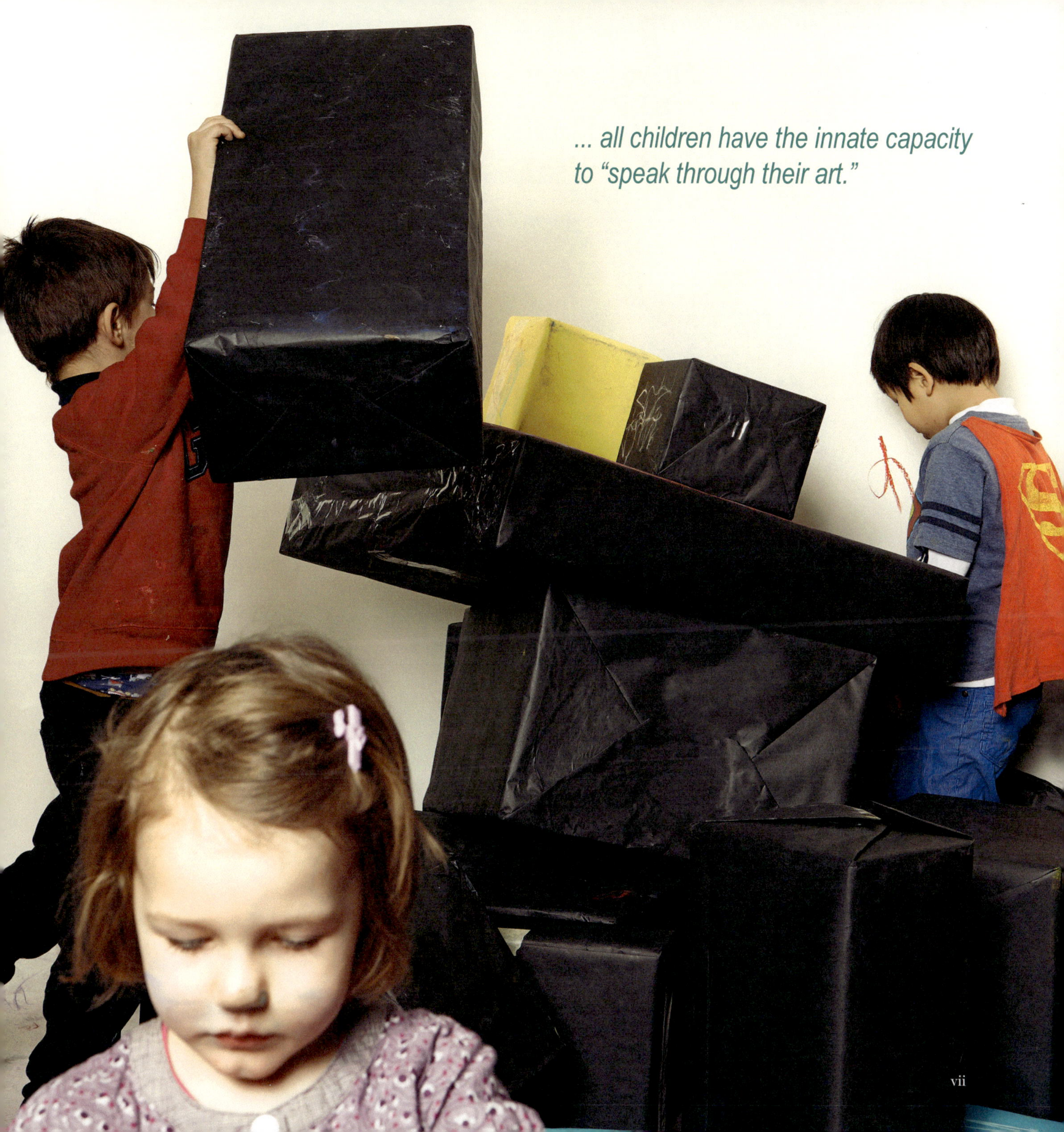
... all children have the innate capacity
to "speak through their art."

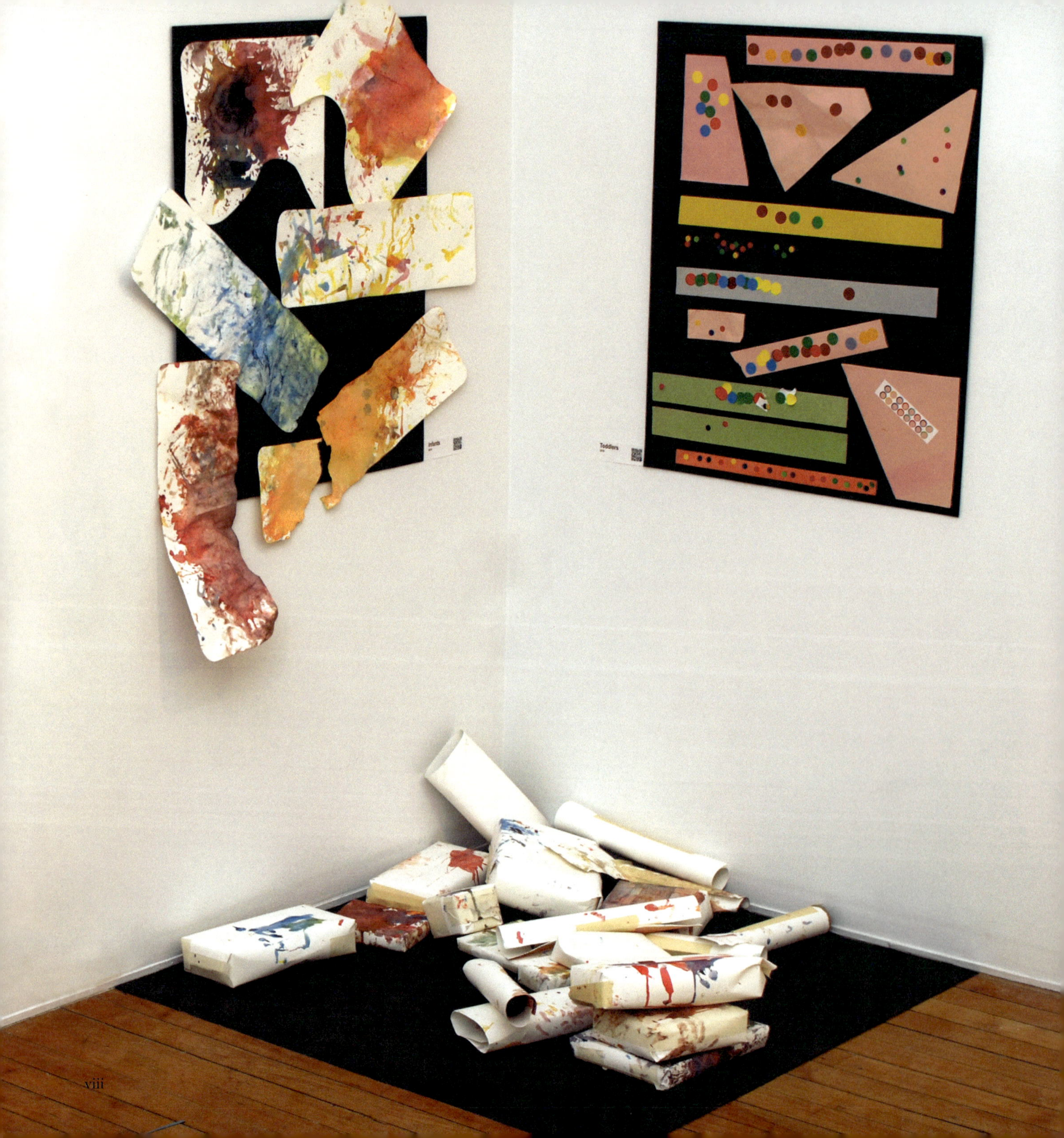

Infants
Toddlers

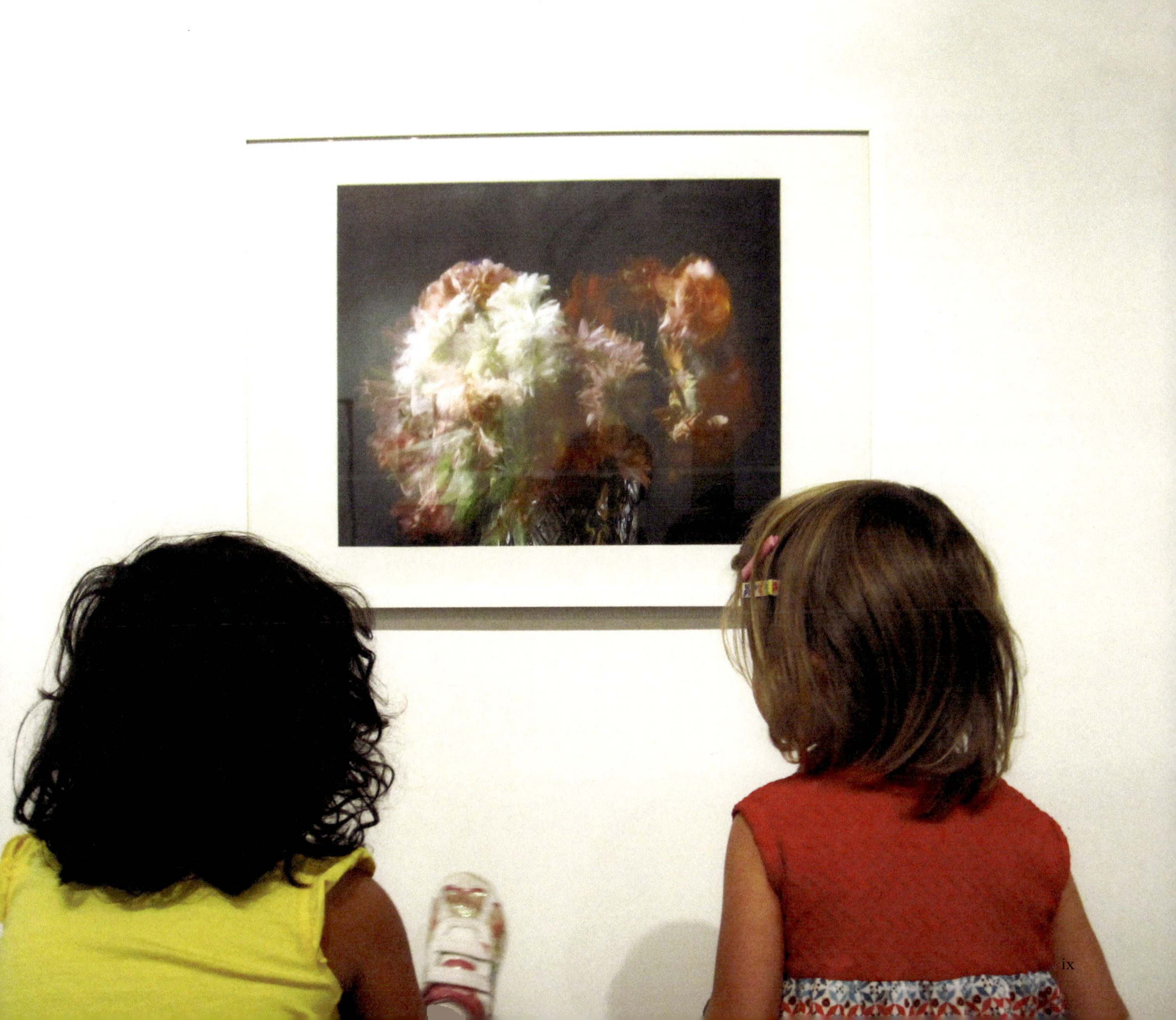

PREFACE

by Susan L. Recchia
Professor and Faculty Director
Rita Gold Early Childhood Center
Teachers College, Columbia University

This year's art show once again demonstrates the intellectual power and artistic beauty that can emerge when infants, toddlers, and preschoolers are given the opportunity to fully participate in expressing their creative ideas in ways that they find meaningful and engaging.

I had the privilege of touring the gallery with Marta Cabral, our curator and art research/teaching fellow, and two delightful toddlers shortly after the art show had been hung. Watching and listening to the children as they re-discovered their own creations and those of their peers, I marveled at the ways they were able to remember what they had done, why they chose particular materials, and what they liked about individual works of art.

Marta's integral role as a participant and guide, not only for the art show but throughout the year, may not be fully visible in the creations on display, as these truly belong to the children. They clearly tell us why they chose to display the items (that we see when asked)—"For my mom" or "I only like red", and how they put them together—"I used glue". Their ownership of their work shines through in their words and actions in response to seeing it all together. When one of the toddlers was asked if a particular drawing was his, he replied, "Yeah, that's me! I made this!" as he traced his finger along the edges with pride.

Each year the art show brings something new and different to the display. This year one of the developing projects used recycled boxes from home as the material of creation. The children painted or decorated the boxes and designed a variety of sculptures with them. Although the boxes were donated by many members of the community and shared by the children, some held particular meaning for individual children as they recognized the container of a familiar food or product from their own homes, a representation of their families' customs.

Marta also introduced a new technology this year, adding scan tags to the children's sculptures which could be accessed using hand held devices. This allowed families and other visitors to the gallery to learn more about the artists' thinking in their own words, previously recorded in a setting that was more comfortable for some of the children.

Our teachers, like Marta, are committed to bringing the children's voices to the fore, giving them ownership or shared ownership whenever possible, and honoring their own ways of knowing, doing, and being.

Watching Marta at work throughout the year, one can't help but see this culminating experience of the art show as also a reflection of her ways of knowing, doing, and being. Marta's work as art teacher, researcher, and curator reflects what we at the Center value as a community and try to instill in every aspect of our work with the children. Ideas and their expression are largely inspired by the children in our setting, where the curriculum is emergent and always in process.

Our teachers, like Marta, are committed to bringing the children's voices to the fore, giving them ownership or shared ownership whenever possible, and honoring their own ways of knowing, doing, and being. This teaching and learning process is a reciprocal one, where both children and teachers learn from and teach each other. It takes place within a caring community, where children's awareness of and respect for others' ideas and feelings is consistently supported.

At one point on our tour, Marta reminds one of the toddlers, whose enthusiastic interest in a peer's work makes it hard not to touch it, "Remember, if you are the artist, you get to decide if it's 'touch art' or 'no touch art' but if the artist is not here, don't touch." Her clear reminders allow the children to make choices not only about what their work will be, but also how they want their work to be shared with others.

As I tour the gallery with the toddlers, I see their delight in finding not only their own creations, but those of their friends. It is fascinating to see how well they know to whom each piece belongs. Alongside their paintings, this year they have taken an odd assortment of recycled materials, or "broken things", and created beautiful artistry that is uniquely their own.

As these two 3-year-old artists, and all of our Center's young artists, engage in the wonders of displaying, sharing, and making more public their art, we see beauty beyond the art itself.

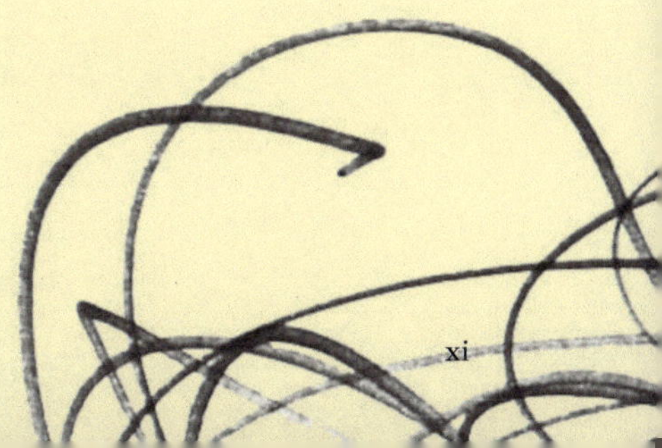

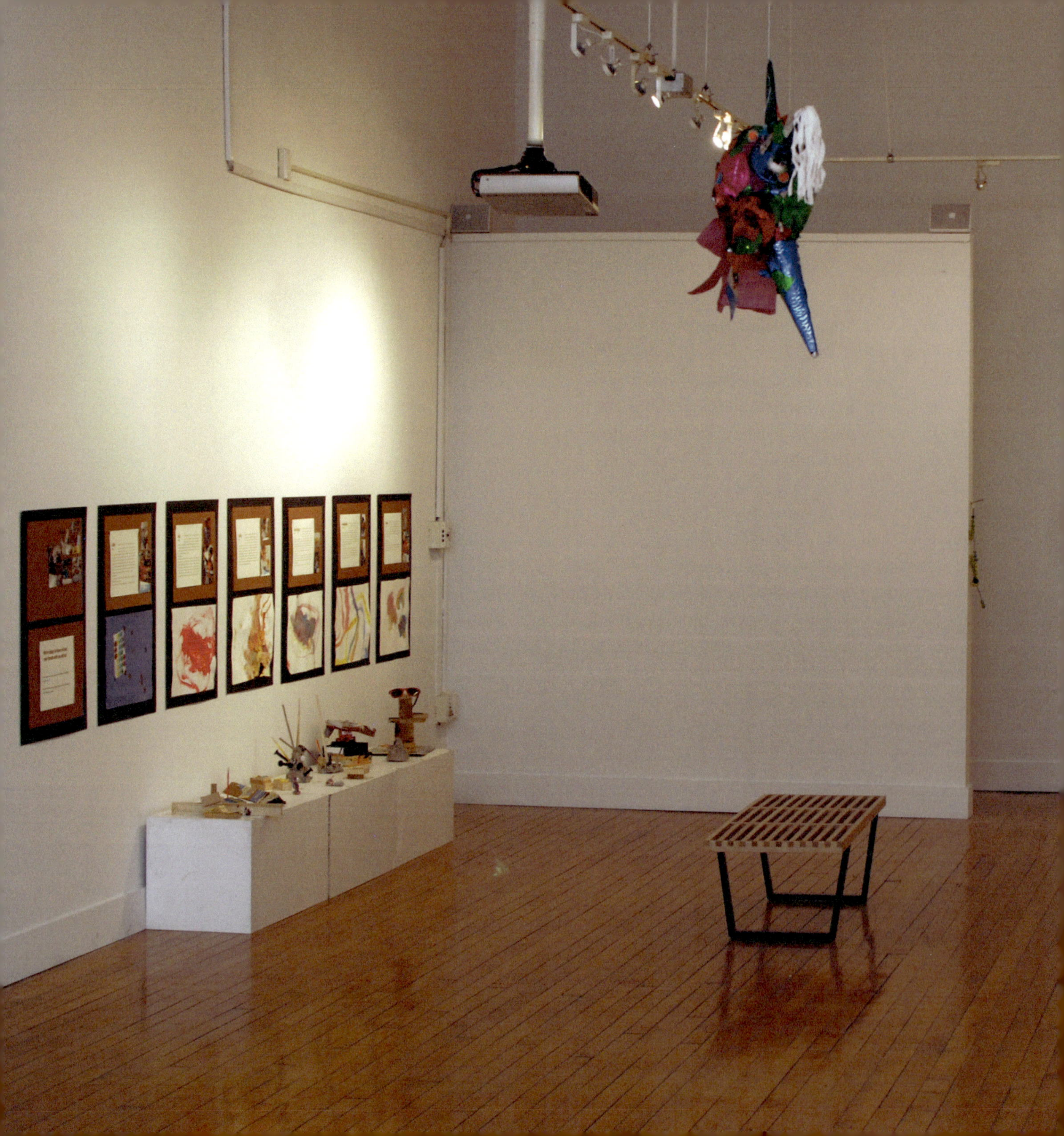

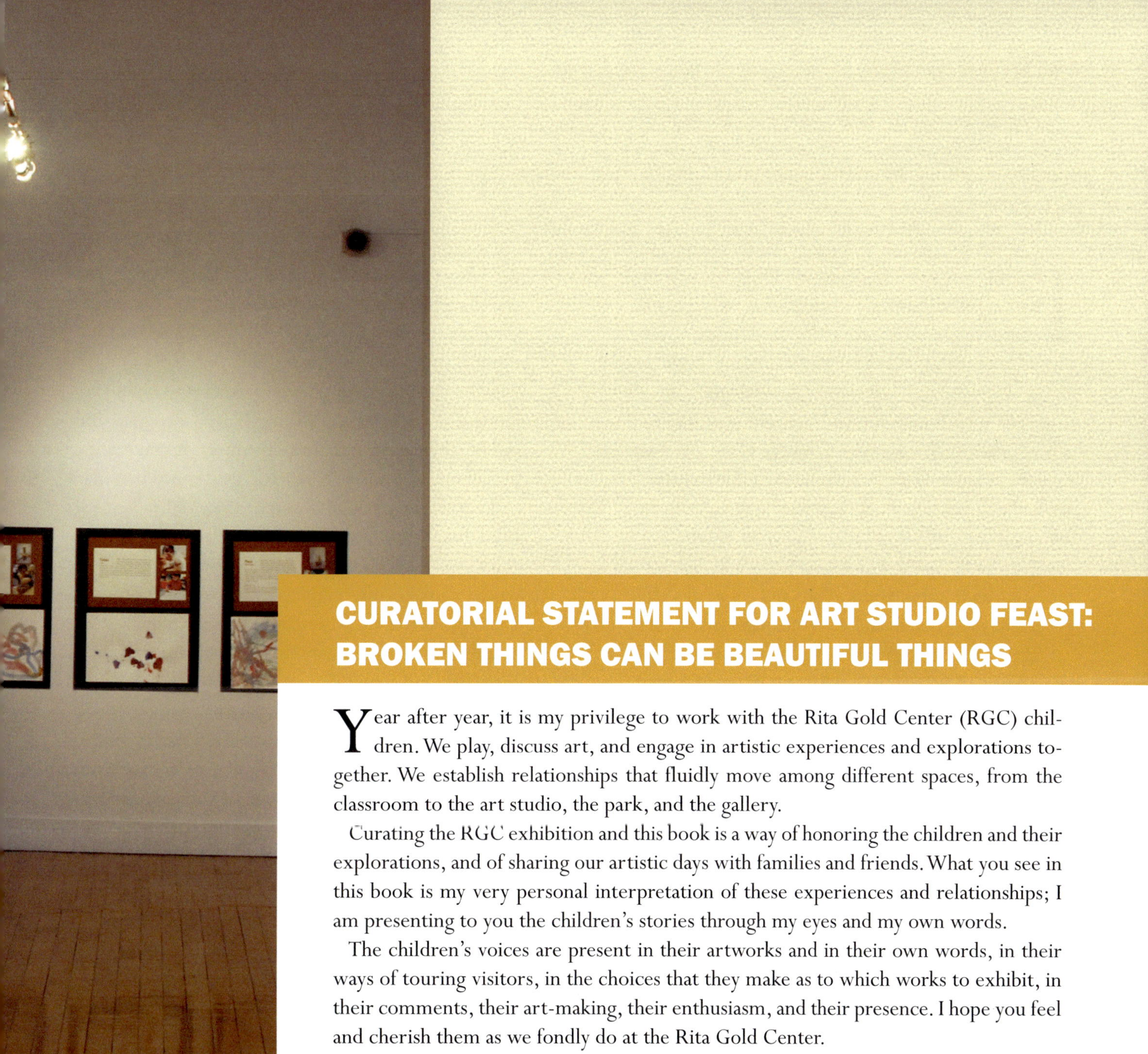

CURATORIAL STATEMENT FOR ART STUDIO FEAST: BROKEN THINGS CAN BE BEAUTIFUL THINGS

Year after year, it is my privilege to work with the Rita Gold Center (RGC) children. We play, discuss art, and engage in artistic experiences and explorations together. We establish relationships that fluidly move among different spaces, from the classroom to the art studio, the park, and the gallery.

Curating the RGC exhibition and this book is a way of honoring the children and their explorations, and of sharing our artistic days with families and friends. What you see in this book is my very personal interpretation of these experiences and relationships; I am presenting to you the children's stories through my eyes and my own words.

The children's voices are present in their artworks and in their own words, in their ways of touring visitors, in the choices that they make as to which works to exhibit, in their comments, their art-making, their enthusiasm, and their presence. I hope you feel and cherish them as we fondly do at the Rita Gold Center.

- Marta Cabral

INTRODUCTION

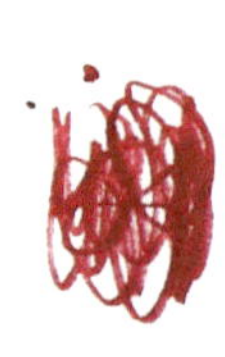

As Haram, Gabriel and I make our way to the art studio, Dylan reaches out to me: "Are you going to have a turn in your home, painting? Me too!" he says, running off to put his boots on to join us.

In many ways, my little art studio at RGC is my home. Technically, my workspace is an old men's restroom, turned into a laundry-storage space, turned into an art studio. Practically, my studio is where I create and keep an organized mayhem of materials with which the children can play and explore. Effectively, this home is where I base my own explorations and questions around children, materials, and art-making; where I think of possibilities for materials, only to let my ideas go when my students come up with their own; where I carefully listen to the children in their explorations and respond as appropriately as I can, in and with the materials we use.

At the RGC, we play. We play a lot. And that playful way of being also guides our artistic explorations and the ways in which we engage with materials, experimenting with the possibilities they offer, and finding new solutions to our questions as well as new questions to our explorations.

Although much of what we do in the RGC art program is based on explorations with materials, looking at and discussing art is also an important and joyful part of it. In the children's artist statements, many references are made to looking at art, and talking about it — and that is indeed an important piece of our artistic experiences at RGC. We visit the Macy Gallery often, where the children and I look at art, discuss it, and are inspired by it. In this context, when time finally comes to install our exhibition, the children have had several experiences in that space and are eager to have visitors looking at and discussing their artworks, in the ways they do with the works of other artists.

Having the opportunity to exhibit children's work in a *real* art gallery is a privilege we enjoy and out of which we try to make the most. It confers the process of the exhibition with a significance that may make it easier for adults to take the children's work in all its seriousness and for the children to own their roles as artists. Having the exhibition up for several weeks provides the children with opportunities to create ways to engage with our guests, guide visitors in tours, and have enough time to truly interact with the show and make it their own. However, as precious an opportunity as exhibiting in a gallery is, the professionalism of the setting is not what gives this show its character. Rather, it is the professionalism with which it is carefully planned, curated, and executed by a team of dedicated and thoughtful people — children and adults — that does.

My role at the Rita Gold Center is not unlike my role in this exhibition and this book: I curate materials and environments that will lead to experiences and explorations and I support the children in their discoveries, sometimes by offering my thoughts and ideas and other times by getting out of the way of *their* thoughts and ideas. I am ever thankful for the possibilities that my position at the RGC opens up to

I curate materials and environments that will lead to experiences and explorations, and I support the children in their discoveries, sometimes by offering my thoughts and ideas and other times by getting out of the way of their thoughts and ideas.

me. me. This role allows me to push my ideas and practices further in a seriously playful environment, learning, and exploring along with my young students.

The Center's staff members are the best of colleagues, and I am very appreciative of all the teachers for the discussions we share, as well as the insights and help they provide me with - and of course for their generosity in letting me be a part of their classrooms and their teaching. A special word of thanks is due to Tran Templeton, my fellow Doctoral Research Fellow at RGC, for being such a wonderful and generous editor of this book and many of my other writings. Many of the Center's families and friends helped in many ways preparing for this exhibition and this book, editing and formatting text, covering boxes and more boxes, taking photos, decorating cake, and doing other small and big tasks. Jueun Yoon, Brianne Smith, and Solange Fingal's help in the community art project for the exhibition's reception featured in this book was equally important. I am very grateful for everyone's joyful enthusiasm and support.

The art exhibition is indeed an important part of my work and a very special occasion for children and families at the Center. The support of the Art and Art Education Program at Teachers College allows us to have the Macy Gallery as an important space in our curriculum year long, and

I thank the program staff for their willingness to serve as visitors in countless guided tours and, most of all, for their patience to have children chatting, drawing, dancing, barking and meowing, marching like dinosaurs, and in so many lively ways occupying the space just outside their offices. The Macy Gallery staff has been incredibly accommodating to the specificities of working with children as artists, 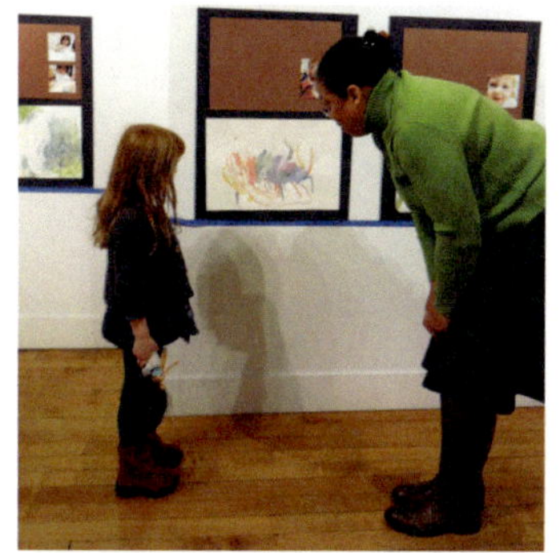 curators, and tour guides, allowing the children's involvement in the process to be taken further and further.

All of this is possible only with the continuous support and encouragement of Judith Burton, Program Director, for whom I am very grateful and appreciative. And, of course, nothing of this could take place without RGC's continual willingness to accommodate and encourage my ideas and my work. I am deeply thankful to our directors Susan Recchia and Patrice Nichols for all their trust and support, and for their generosity in cherishing and cheering on my practices and my ideas – my work as it is could not be done without their support.

INFANTS

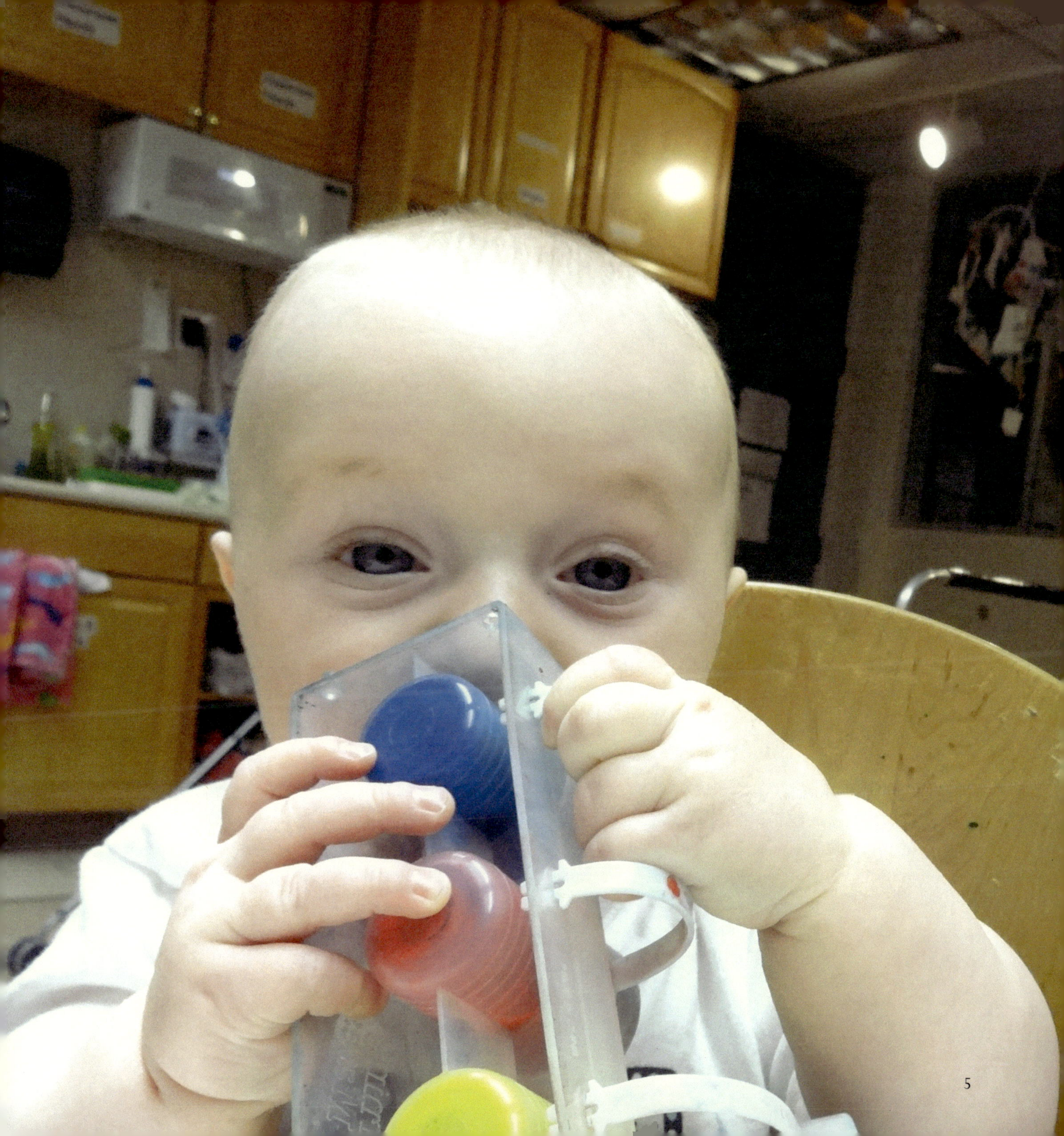

CALLIE

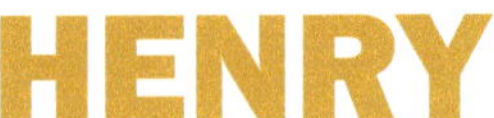

HENRY

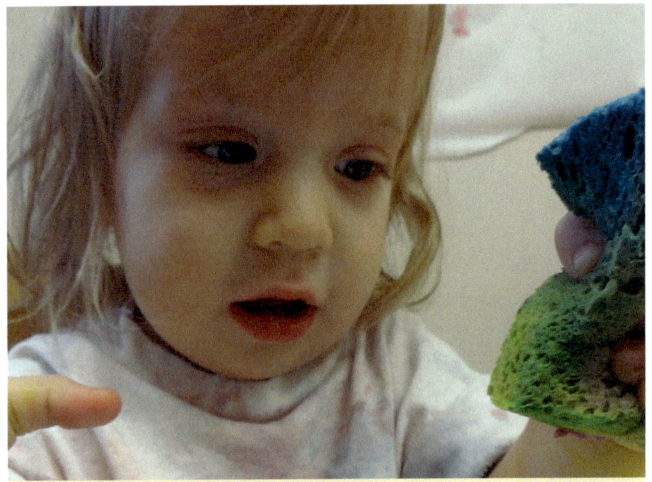

An enthusiastic painter, Henry enjoys the feeling of paint on his hands. He seems to be excited when he casually pours paint on his paper by shaking the containers, and makes eye contact with his teacher to share the news.

Henry holds his brush and explores it with his hands and mouth, feeling the texture of the bristles. He smiles joyfully throughout his painting endeavors.

A determined and fearless artist, Callie knows what she wants in her art making. When painting, she makes her choices of paper and brush, and gets to work using her hands and all her tools to make marks on the paper. She smilingly observes how the watercolor paint spreads over the paper when she pours it and splashes when she taps it, and she asks for more paints so that she can repeat her experimentations.

Callie likes to fold her paper, tear it in small pieces, and make holes in it. Sometimes she tears large sections of her paper and throws them to the floor, refusing to take them back as she holds on to the pieces she chooses to keep. Callie pays close attention to her paintings, and after a moment of intense observation, sometimes gives them a kiss.

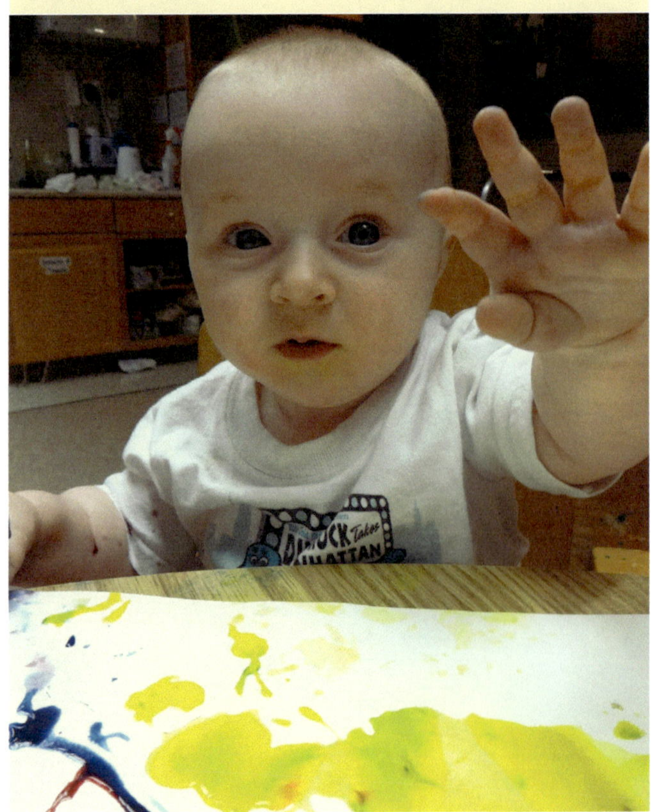

NOAM

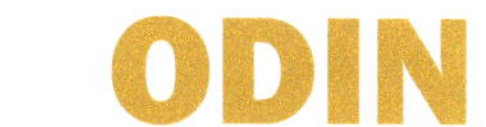

ODIN

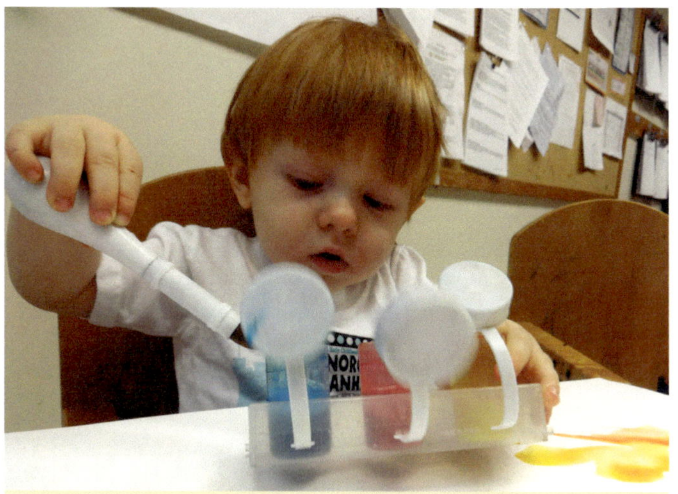

O din enjoys his painting explorations, and carefully touches the paint with the tip of his fingers first, and then his whole hand. He is surprised by the result of his actions when he pours the paint on the paper and watches it spread with the colors mixing on the paper.

When he playfully taps his hands on the paint and it splashes out, Odin is surprised and not so happy when it lands on his face, but soon realizes it's okay and resumes his explorations.

A playful artist, Noam likes to incorporate toys in his artistic explorations as part of his mark-making narrative. He uses his toys to play with the paint, as he does with his tools, pushing his watercolor containers on his paper like cars or trains. While painting, he often makes noises that match his play.

Noam enjoys swishing the paint from side to side with his sponge, and he observes the paint carefully as it spreads on the paper when poured – asking for more paints to see that the same action of pouring will have the same result of paint spreading. Rather than using his hands, he prefers to use his paintbrush as a tool for mark-making, particularly when engaging in side-to-side swiping motions, and he often chooses to paint with its wooden end. Noam also enjoys playing with clay, customarily using toys in his explorations.

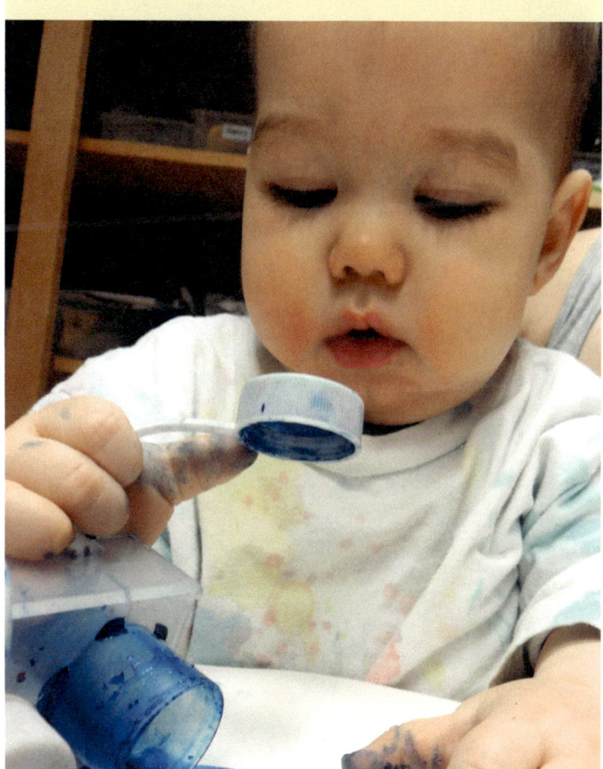

SAHANA

In her painting, Sahana often uses her fingers as tools. She likes to use her paintbrush as part of the process, dipping it in the paint, putting the paint on her finger, and then using her finger to make marks on her paper. She likes to use both ends of her paintbrush to make marks.

Sahana asks for the tools and materials she needs, and makes choices in the process. She often asks for yellow, sometimes using it as the main color in her paintings. When looking at her paintings, Sahana often points out colors and marks for her teachers to comment on, with an apparent preference for yellow.

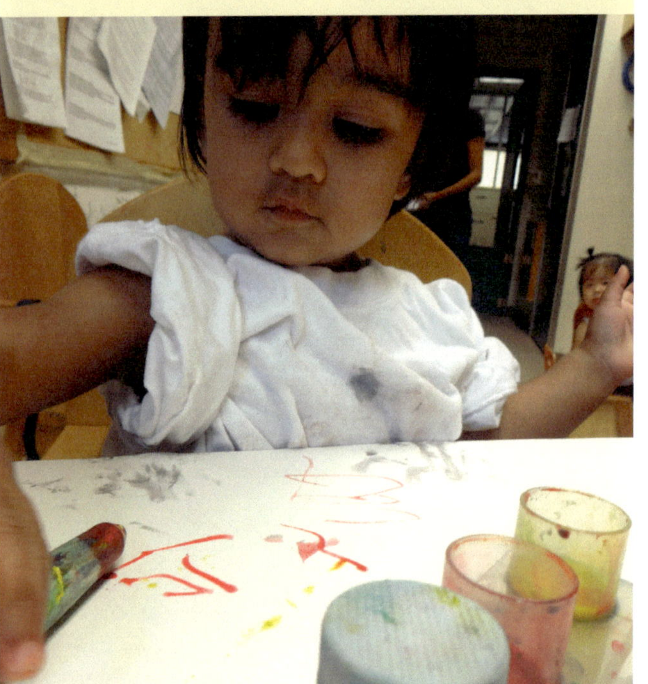

SEUNGHA

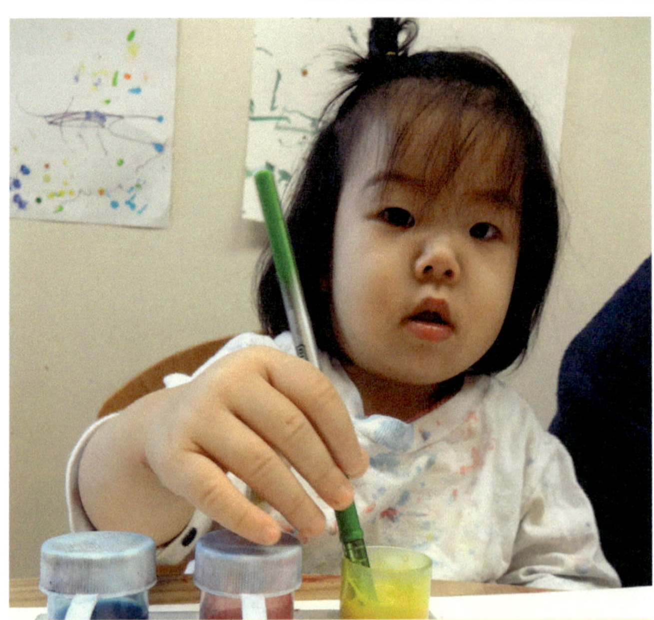

Seungha is curious about the art materials presented to her in the classroom, and likes to take her time to observe what is going on before engaging with her hands. She decides how she wants her paper to be placed and what kind of paintbrush she wants to use. She carefully notices the results of her actions when she makes marks with the paint or scratches on the paper with her fingernails or paintbrush.

Seungha enjoys painting on paper and on boxes, and likes to use toys as mark-making tools. Seungha also enjoys clay. She seems to be curious about it as a material, and likes to touch and manipulate her clay using both hands to grab, tap, and poke.

TULASI

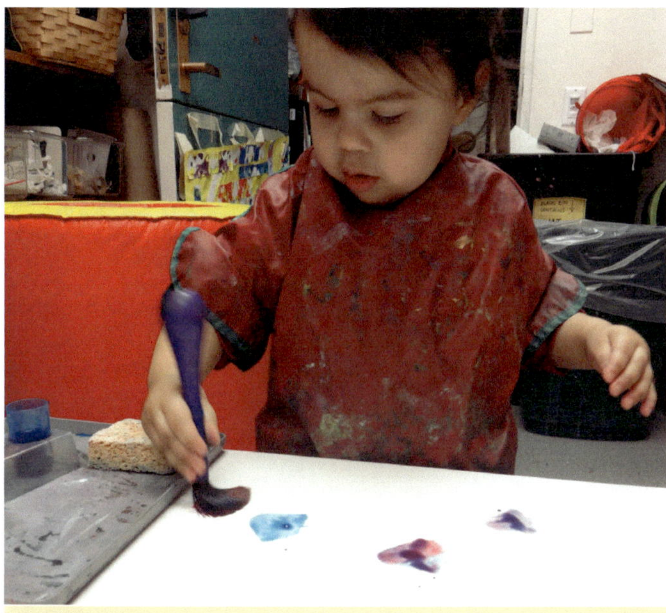

Tulasi is a determined artist. She likes to explore different uses of her tools, and eagerly uses both ends of her paintbrushes to make marks on the paper. She enjoys ripping and pulling pieces of paper from her painting, using stickers and other materials. Tulasi enjoys going to the art studio and likes to paint standing up by the table, using her watercolors, brush, sponge, and water. She attentively observes the marks her paintbrush leaves on the paper, then looks closely at the brush itself that she holds in her hand.

Tulasi takes the time to observe her paintings when she is done, and studies the colors, marks, and lines that are pointed out to her during conversations around her work.

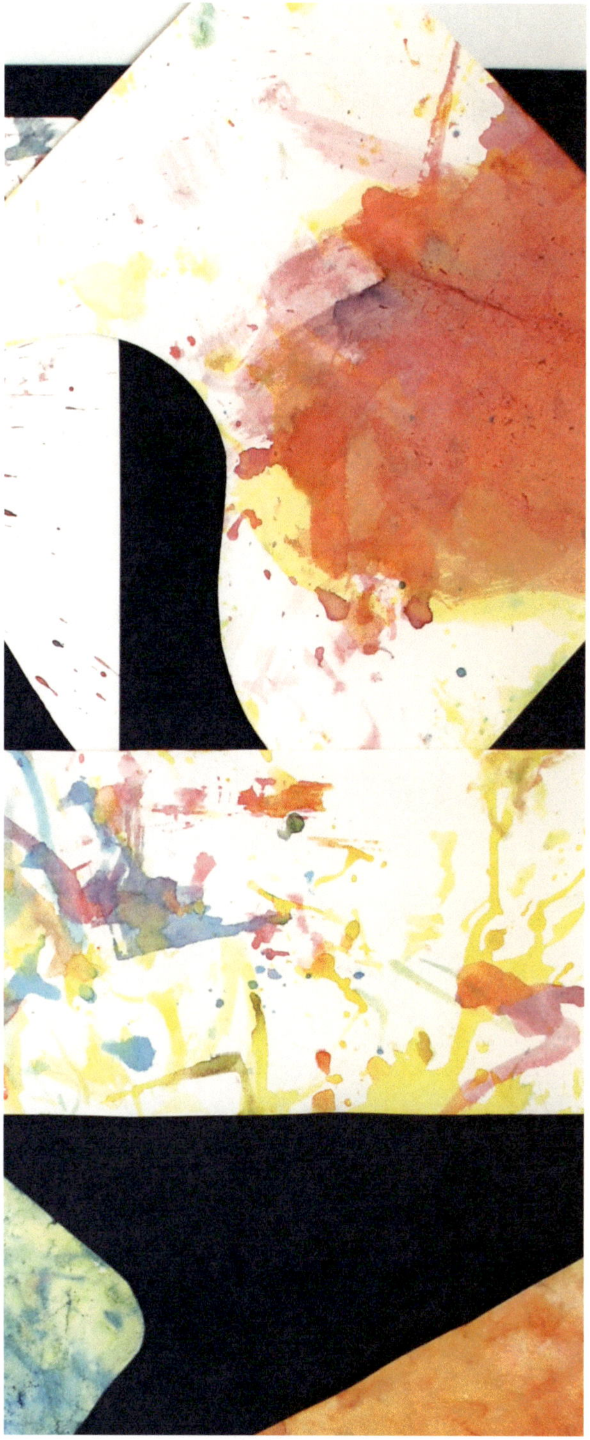

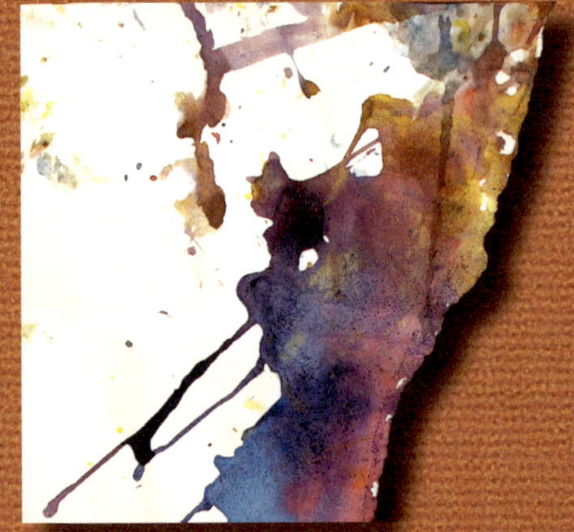

CALLIE

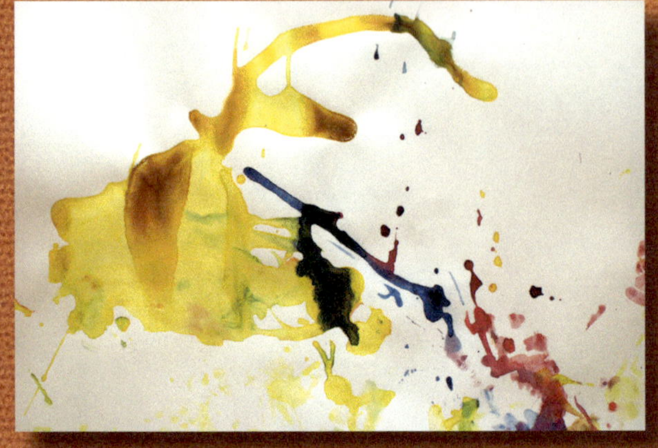

HENRY

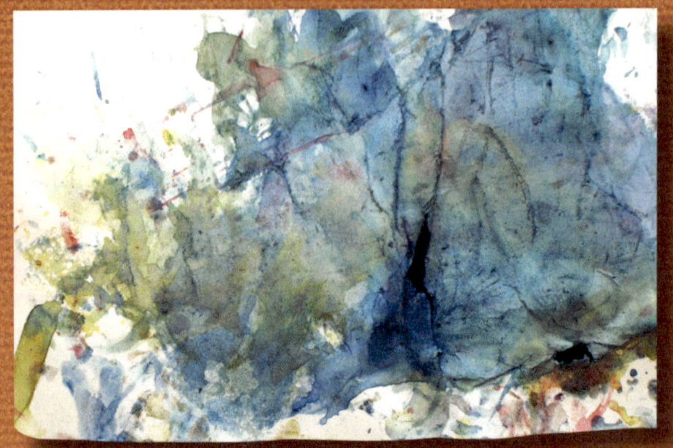

NOAM

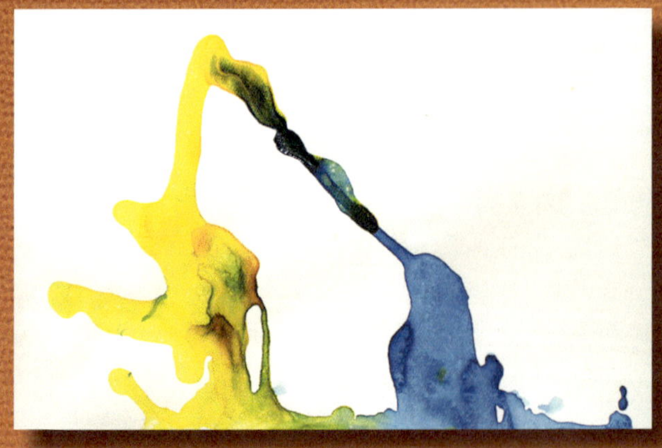

ODIN

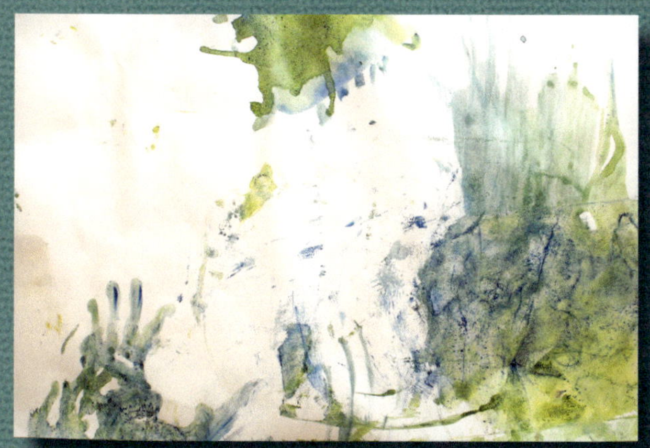

SAHANA

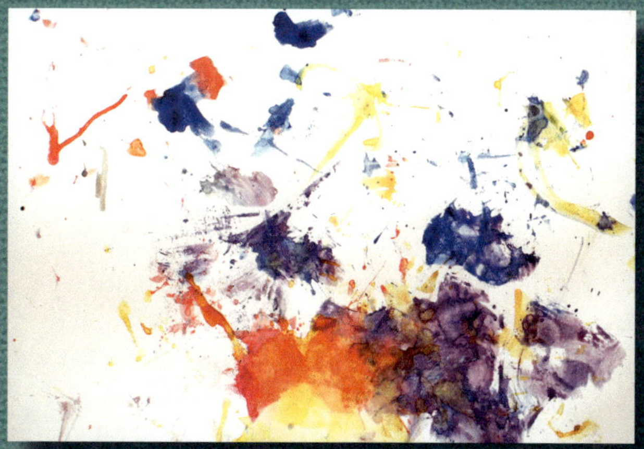

SEUNGHA

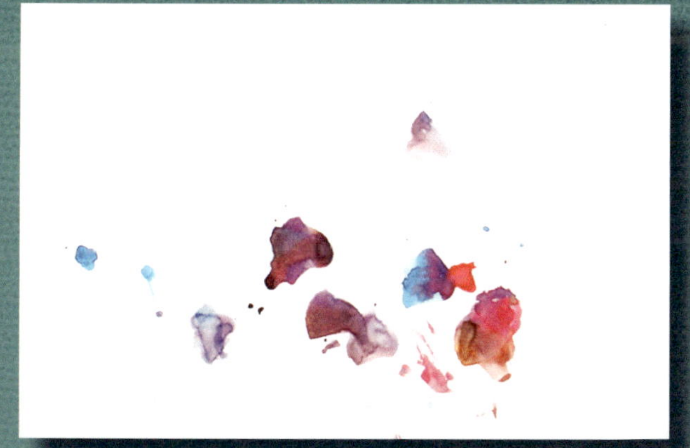

TULASI

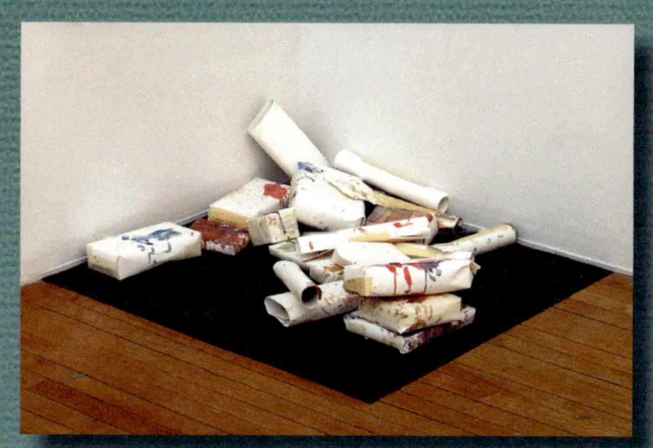

INFANTS

BROKEN THINGS

"I like broken things, because broken things can be beautiful," *Sophia says as we work on her artist statement. I agree.*

Stepping into the RGC, we are welcomed by a couple of empty boxes, where anyone may leave random objects as donations – corks, leftover paper, old keys, objects that were to be thrown away – that can be used as art materials. Found objects are an important part of the studio art program at the Center: even though "broken things" turned out to be a very present part of this year's art exhibition, working with re-purposed objects is not something we did specifically for this show, but rather a practice I try to bring to the Center in my daily work.

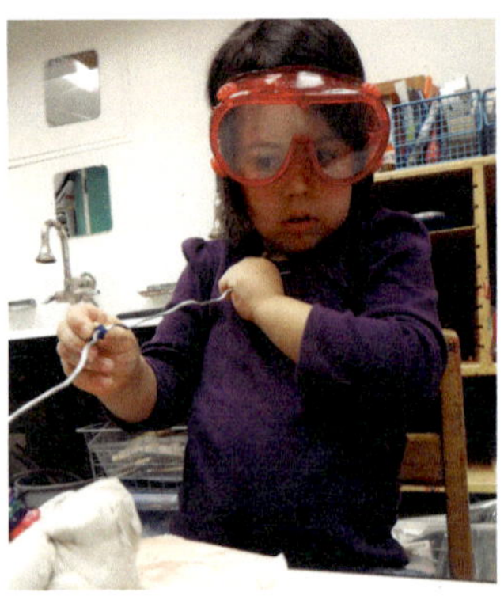

As I collect diverse and numerous materials myself and encourage families and staff to do the same, I organize the materials and make them available in our tiny studio. The children often enthusiastically participate in this process of sorting objects, and quickly become familiar with the magical joy of digging into a box of random objects and being inspired by what we find. Looking at an old single slipper, broken sunglasses, a twig, half a cork, or an old paintbrush, children find new uses for objects that usually are taken to have very specific – and specified – purposes, and transform them as part of 3D collages and other works.

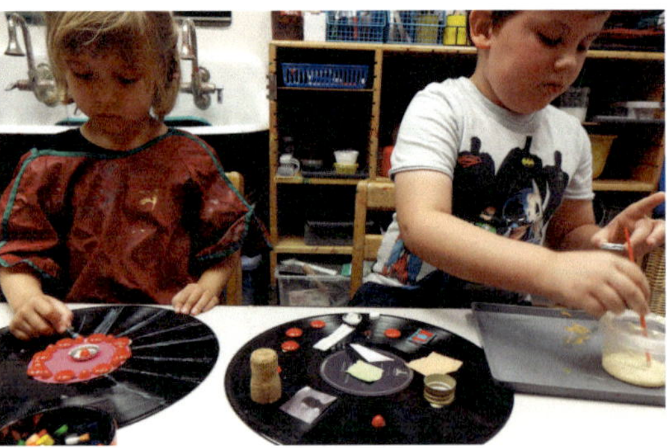

As children get used to "looking at things as if they could be otherwise"[1], they are encouraged to bring those practices to their classrooms and their daily experiences, eventually developing ways of looking at their surroundings, ways that may embrace that flexibility, essentially cultivating "multiple ways of seeing and multiple dialogues in a world where nothing stays the same"[2].

---

1   Greene, M. (1995. p. 16). *Releasing the imagination: Essays on education, the arts, and social change.* San Francisco: Jossey-Bass.

2   Ibid.

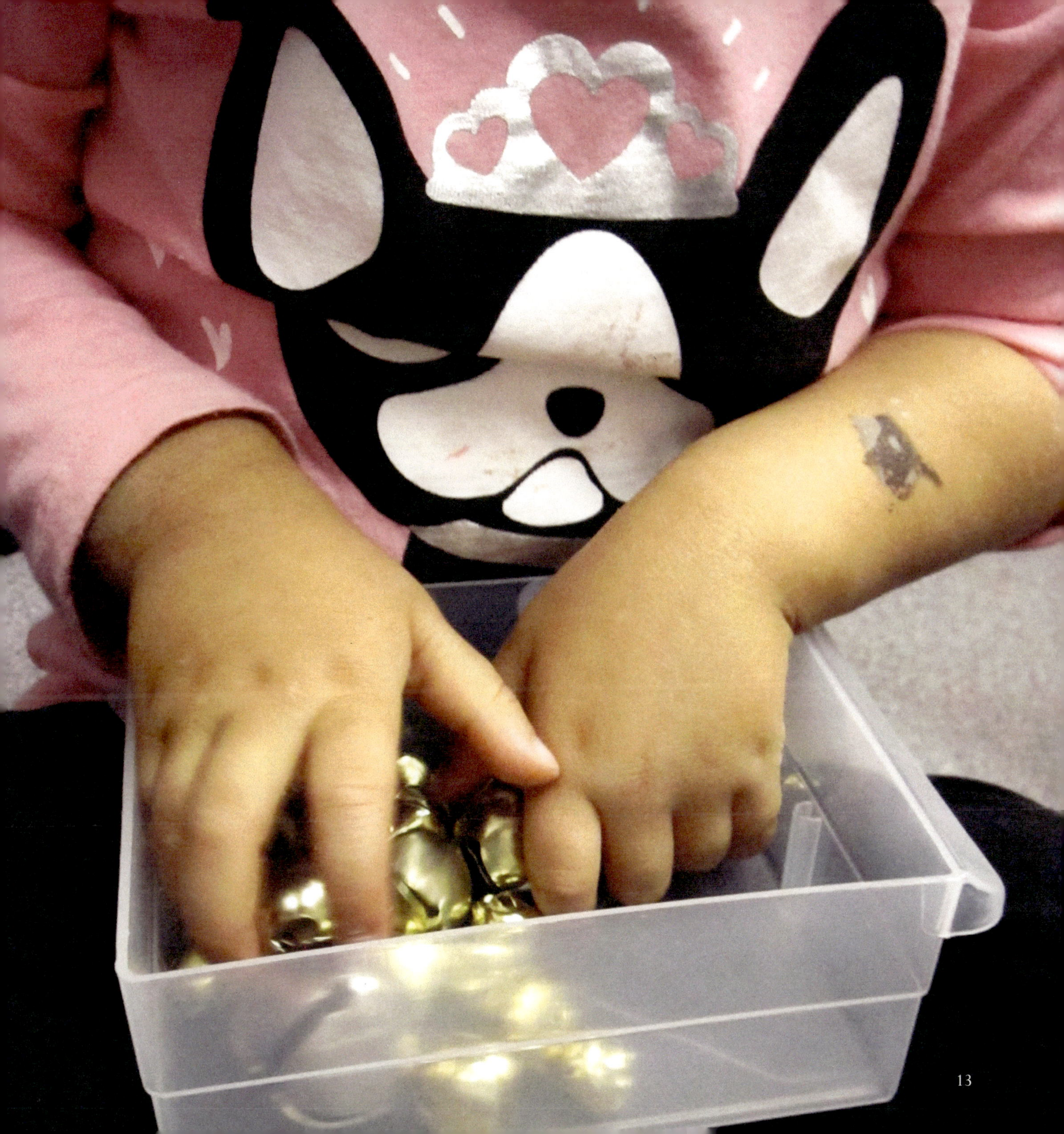

TODDLERS

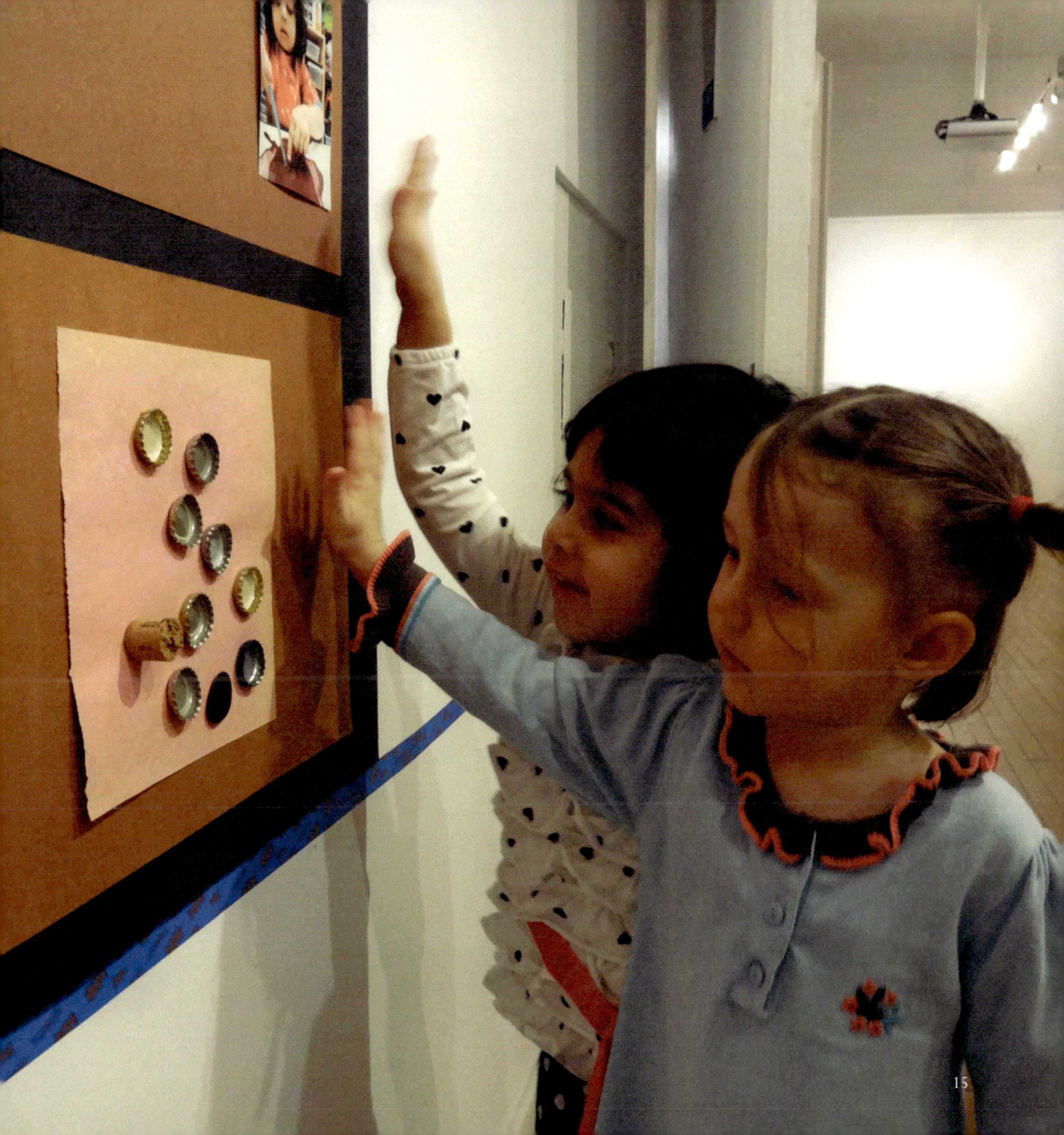

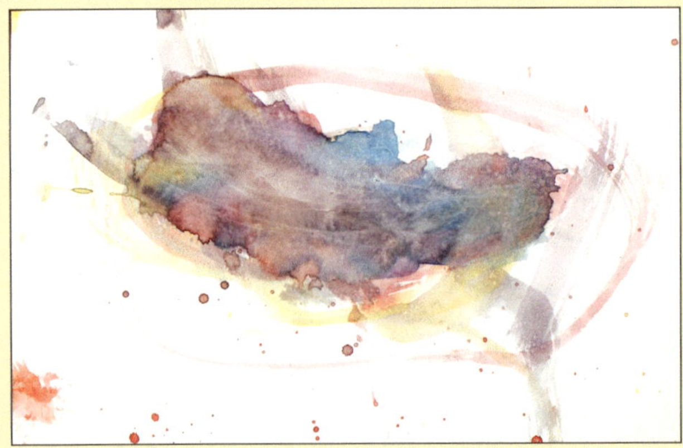

CLARA

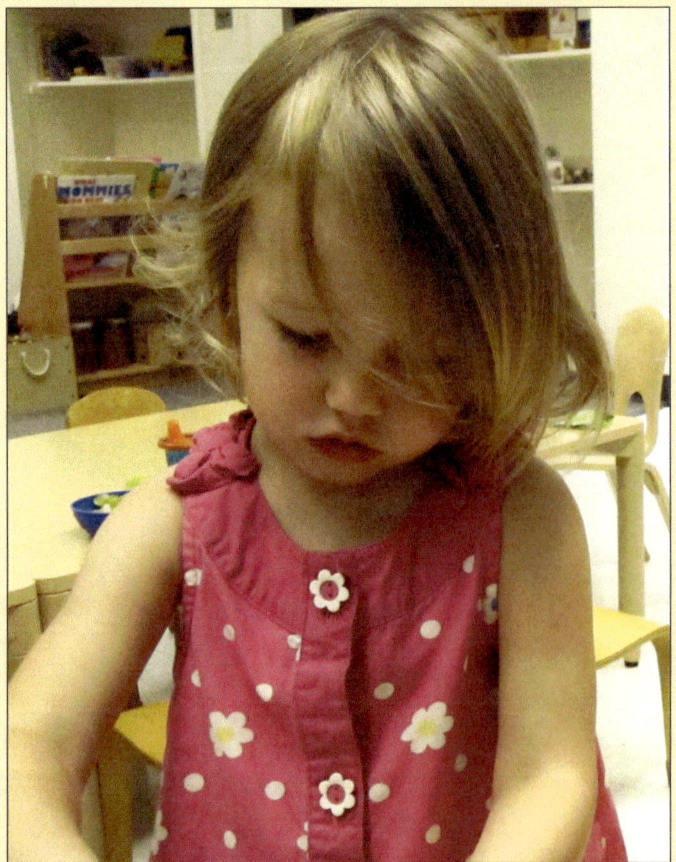

ABOUT THE ARTIST

As she was selecting the works she wanted to exhibit, Clara took her time to closely look at her art before she made her decision. This is not unusual for her – a thoughtful artist, Clara often stops to pay close attention to artworks and comment on them, be they her own creations or other works she sees in the art gallery or studio. But it is not all about the talking: Clara likes to explore a variety of materials, building on her prior knowledge about them to find new and sometimes unexpected ways of pushing her experimentations further. Clara knows what she wants, and is not afraid to ask for assistance when she needs it: "I need a new paper. I need a new brush - cause look, I'm making thick." Any sort of assistance, really: "Marta, can you come over here and I can put peanut butter [clay] on you?"

IN HER OWN WORDS

I'm three. I like to paint on paper. I like to use purple and pink and I like red and white and black and blue. I like the buttons. I have two cats. When they go outside I pick them up back into the house and then when I go back here to art studio I tell all about my paintings because it's everyone's painting in the art studio.

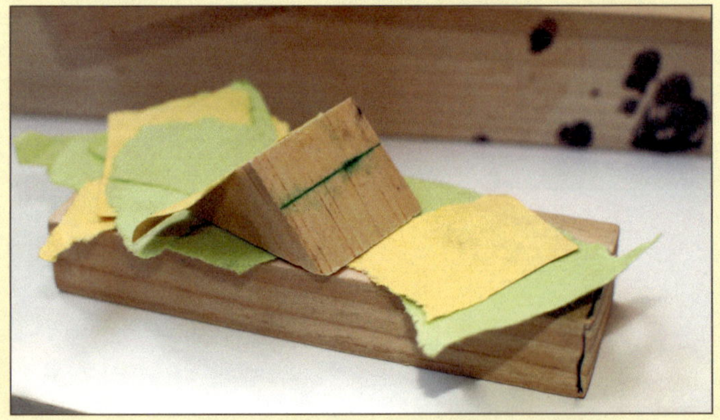

CLARA

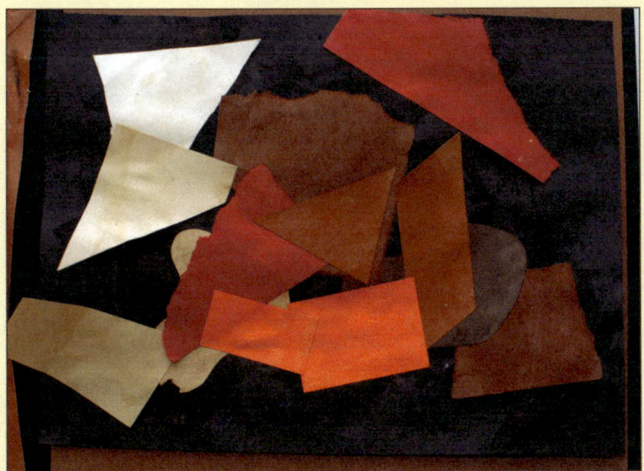

This is mine. I made it! I made Mama and my Papa.

ABOUT THE ARTIST

Clara likes to be hands-on with the materials more than she likes talking about it. "I wanna work! I wanna work!" she says when asked about her artwork. A joyful artist, Clara often sings while she paints. Her family is a constant source of inspiration and exclamations - "Mommy! Daddy! Mommy! Daddy! And my sister!" often accompany her explorations. A fan of 2D collage, Clara likes to keep her hands clean and often calls out "hands!" when she wants to wipe them. When painting, Clara likes to experiment with different brushes and oftentimes chooses to work with two brushes at once, either one in each hand or the two together in one hand: "I need two! Two brushes! More! Look, look! I like it!"

IN HER OWN WORDS

I like to paint. I want to paint! I want to paint! Go with Marta!

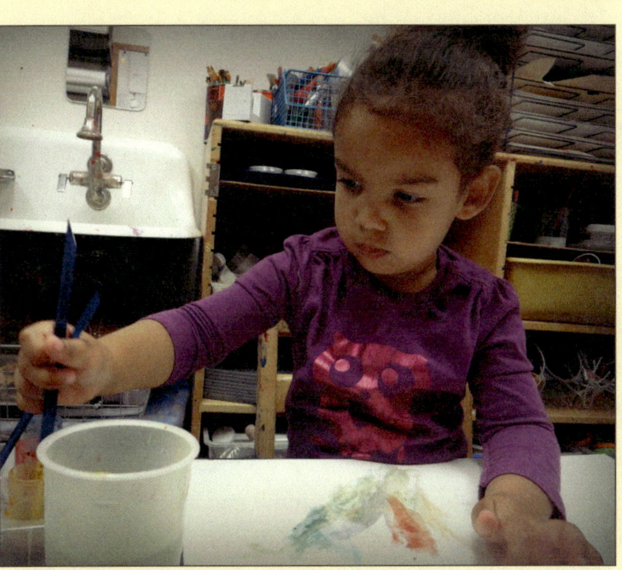

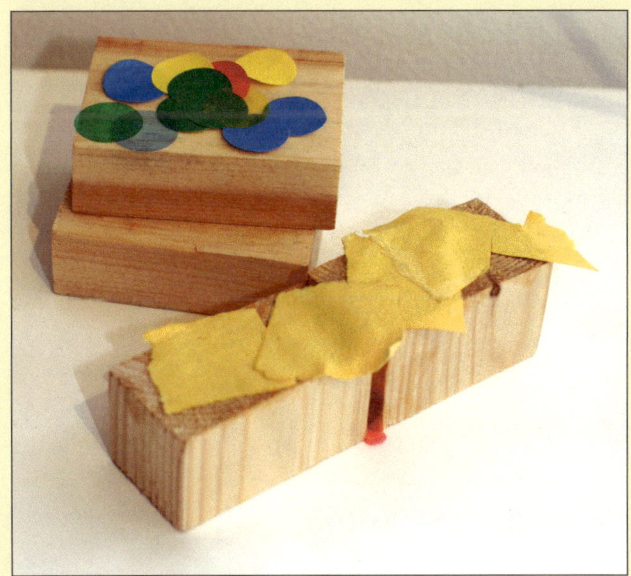

Stickers! Two stickers. I like blues ones.

ABOUT THE ARTIST

Hari approaches his color mixing with intensity and precision, as he concentrates in understanding his own experimental processes. "I'm putting the blue into the red! I'm melting it! It's making purple! When you mix blue, it makes purple!," he reasons. But different days call for different colors, and the explorations continue: "See, that makes orange! You mix yellow with red, and it makes orange." When he notices something special in someone else's color, Hari asks about it: "I want brown too, how did that happen [to your color]?

IN HIS OWN WORDS

I call this a sculpture. [I want to have this one in the art show] because I made it big and I want to show Mommy how big it is. I put a big block on the bottom and then little blocks on the top to make a big tower. I used glue because I wanted to stick it together. If I don't use glue, it falls down. I used paint with different colors. Blue in the bottom, red on the tops. I mixed the purple with the blue and red. I put a lot of paint on the bottom because I wanted it to be beautiful for Mommy to see it. Where's the pudding box? The pudding box is right there.

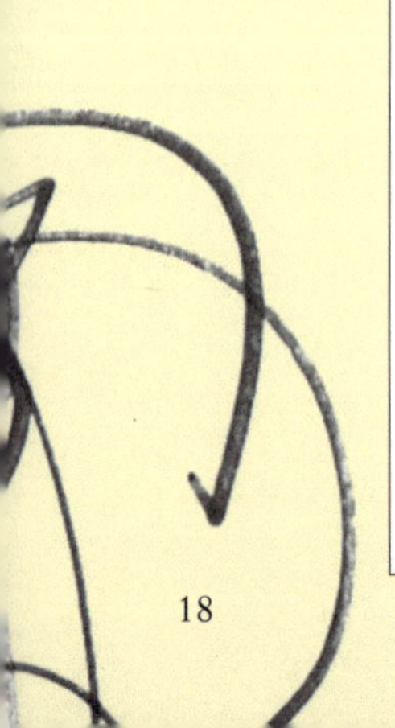

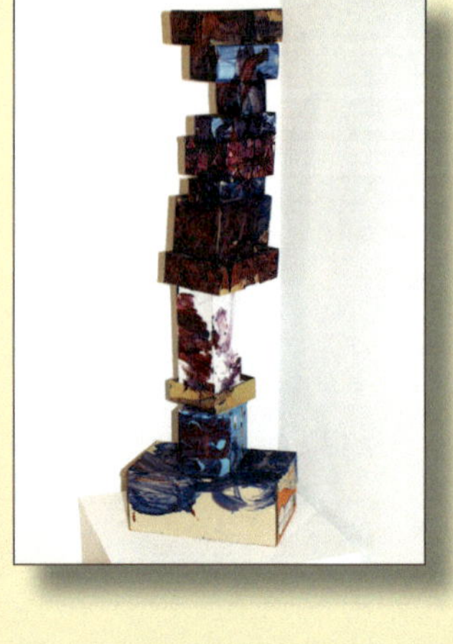

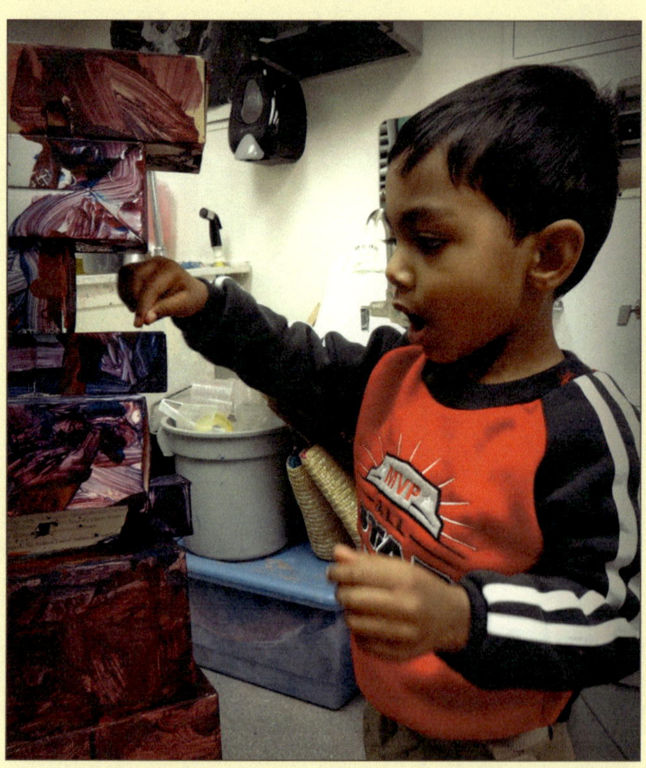

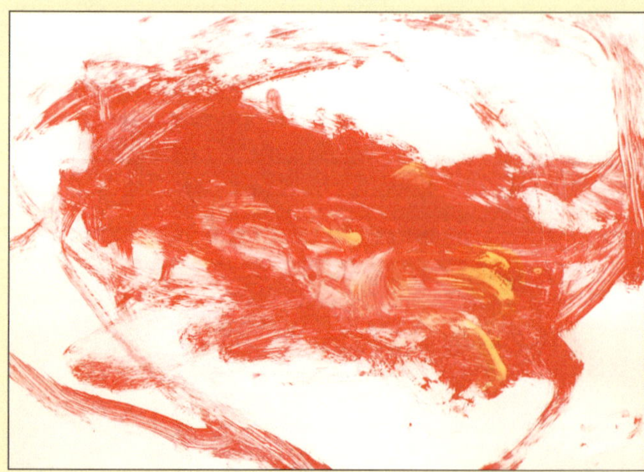

[I choose] this one because I like red.

ABOUT THE ARTIST

Hiwa's interest in cooking often shows up in her art. She works her clay into pancakes and strawberries, and ice cream is a frequent source of inspiration for the narratives she creates around her work with materials. Playing with her clay, Hiwa enjoys breaking it into tiny little pieces that she then arranges on the table in front of her. She creates "strawberries," to later mash back together into "pancakes" that she shares with her friends. "I need to make food! Food clay," she states. Hiwa knows her tools well, and when painting, she likes to explore what different brushes can do, naming the round, flat, and fan brushes as she picks them.

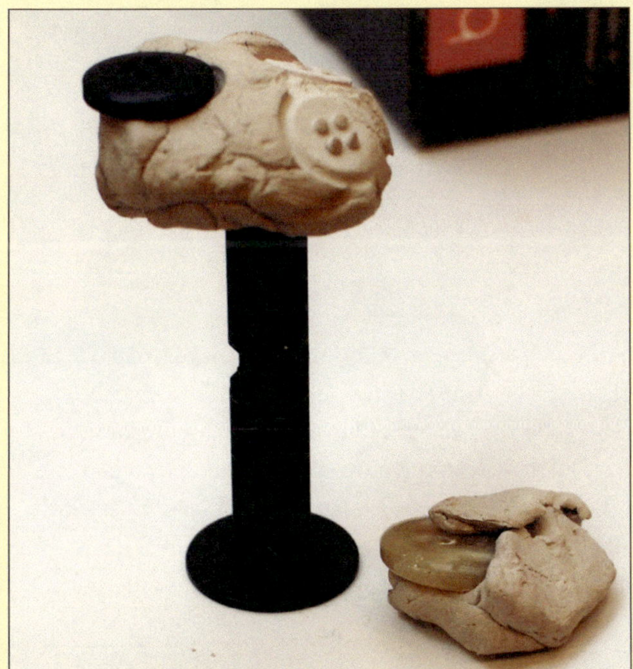

This is kind of sticky clay. I like to cut it up. With a knife and I make something with buttons on it so my dad can know that I made this clay cause I made this button.

HIWA

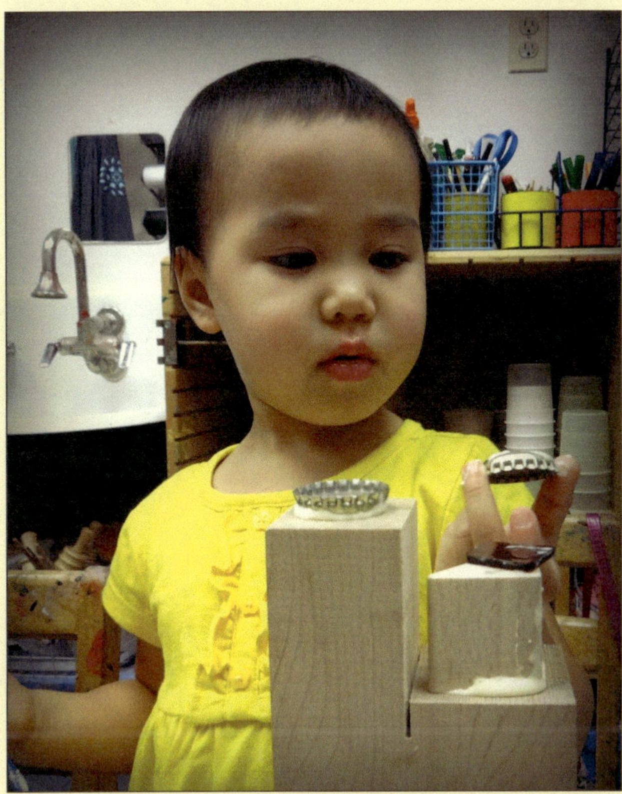

This is for you! Just for you! You're lucky to have clay for yourself. I have a little special clay for your artwork, just for you.

IN HER OWN WORDS

I like to paint. With pink. Pink is my favorite. And peach. Bailey [Hiwa's sister] is my little munchkin. Bailey came out of Mommy's tummy. My daddy is my boulou. I'm three. I'm an artist. I do some clay, some button on clay.

I color with paint.

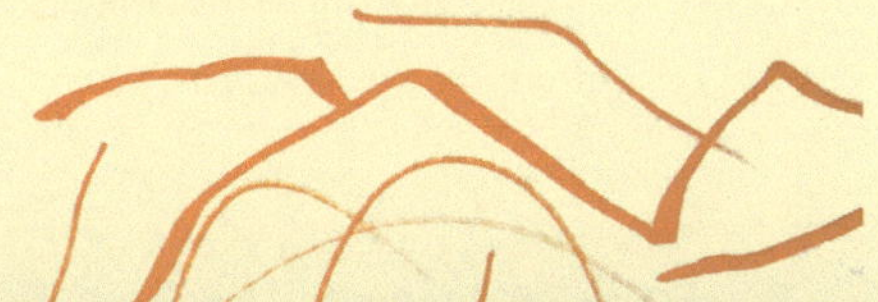

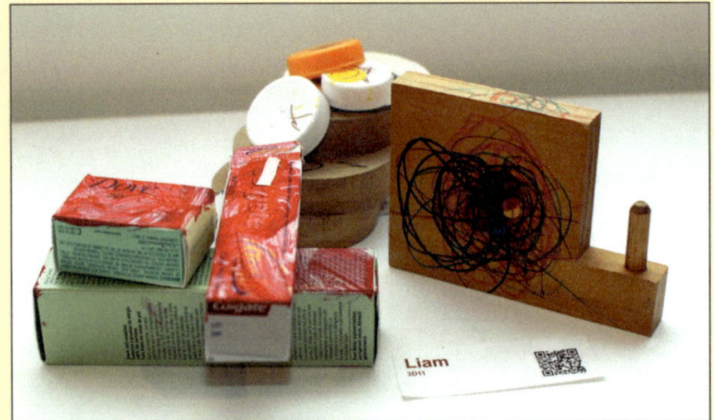

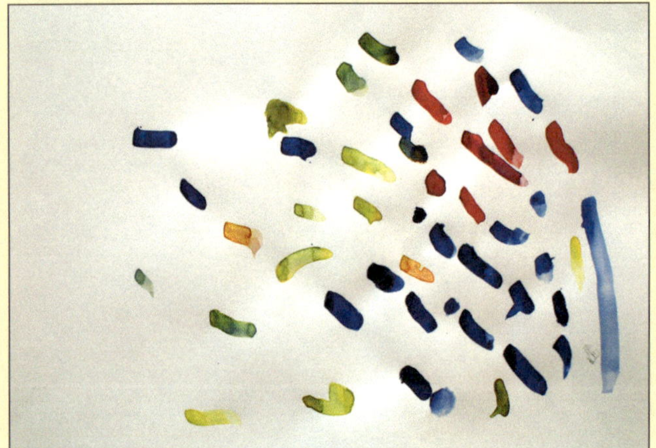

LIAM

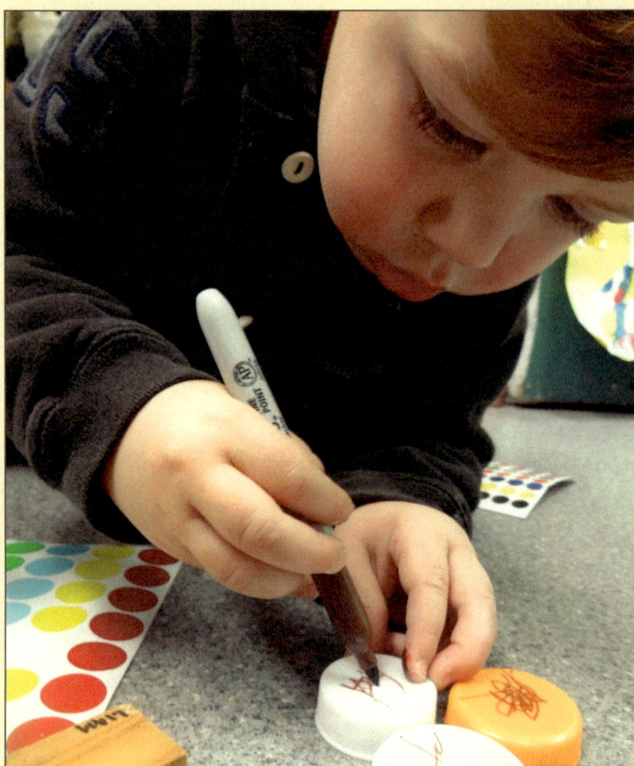

ABOUT THE ARTIST

When asked what he likes to do in the art studio, Liam decisively points to paints and brushes. Indeed, he is an enthusiastic painter who likes to share his joy by voicing out: "Apple! Apple! Mama!"

Liam makes decisions as to what paintbrush he wants and how his paper should be positioned. He is clear in letting his teachers know when something else catches his eye and he wants to move on to other explorations.

2D and 3D collage are also amongst Liam's favorite activities, and he enjoys working with boxes, wood, and other materials. He is always ready to work in the art studio, making sure he makes that clear whenever he foresees an opportunity for a visit.

When selecting his artworks for this exhibition, Liam was determined in the way he picked up some of his paintings and refused others, as he did with his 3D works — he picked up and played with the wood, stickers, and bottle cap piece, while pushing away his other 3D collage, while distinctly saying, "No!"

IN HIS OWN WORDS

Apple! Apple! Blue!

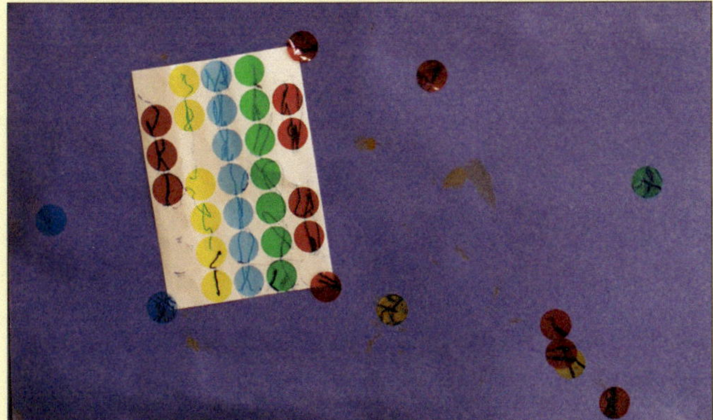

LILLIAN

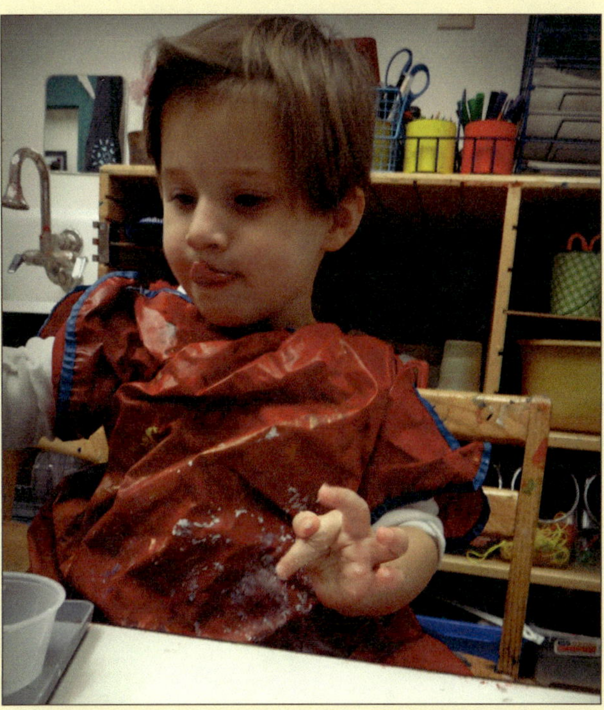

ABOUT THE ARTIST

Lillian is a fearless artist. She likes to explore innovative ways of using materials and has a special fondness for sensory experiences and materials like glue, clay, and paint. Glue is one of her favorite materials, and Lilly likes to drop beads and small pieces in it, fishing them out with her hands later on. She often shares with her peers her knowledge of this particular material and the specific possibilities it offers. "Clay dirty is really good!" Lillian says, actively studying her clay by squishing, pounding, and sliding, using her whole body's strength for the "clay mess good mess." But it is not always about getting messy, and Lilly sometimes takes the initiative to keep it tidy, explaining it: "I'm not messing up. No, not on the floor. There's no paint on the floor, I'm watching what I'm doing, I'm not just messing around with things and putting things in my head."

IN HER OWN WORDS

I like to play and dance. I like glue. I like the corners of the paper sticky. I like to make art with my friends. My favorite color is purple.

I did this one. Because I did all these circles right here. I make it stay with stickers.

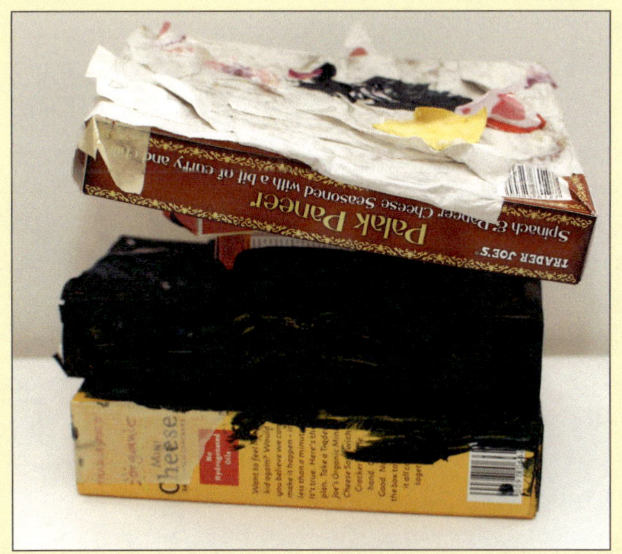

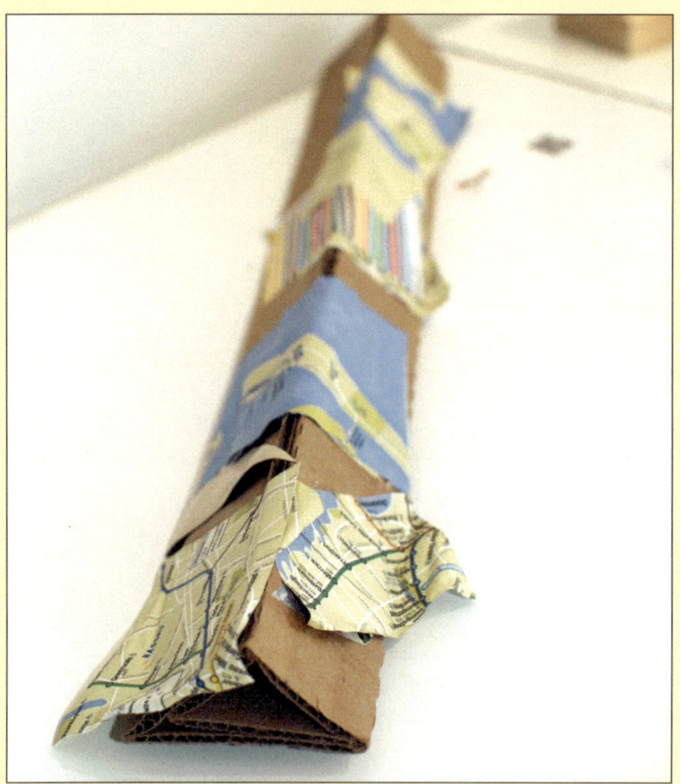

MIGUEL

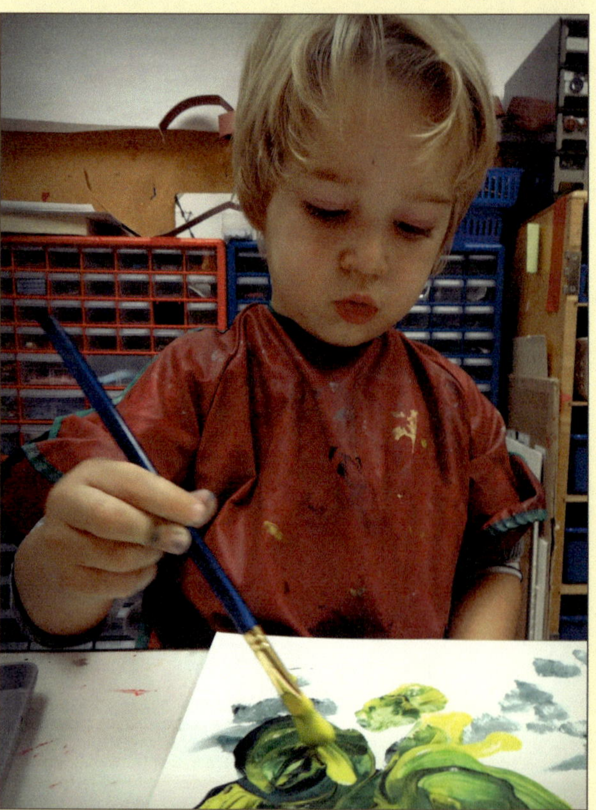

ABOUT THE ARTIST

Miguel is exuberant in his artistic explorations and embraces new and known materials with enthusiasm. He often shares his discoveries with a loud "Taran!" as he makes a new mark or somehow changes his material. While looking at his artworks, Miguel smiles and nods to himself: "Huhum!" Miguel likes to work with different materials, often showing a preference for clay and painting.

IN HIS OWN WORDS

I like clay. Painting. Blue. [I like to make art with] only Miguel. I like to make a car. I used paper, glue. Sticky. A paper inside! [Pulling out a little piece of yellow paper from inside, Miguel picked his work from an assortment of others.]

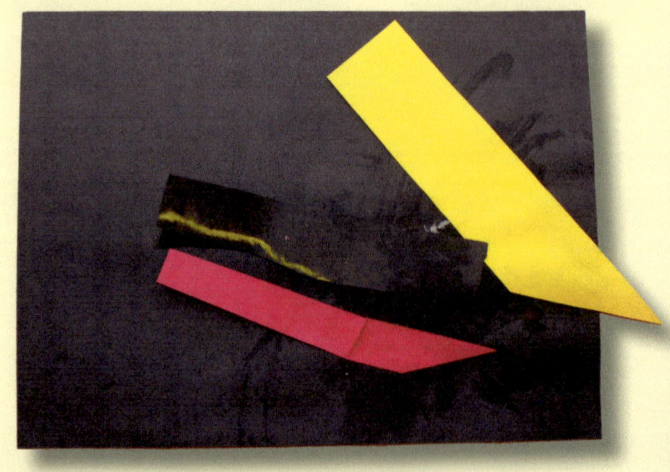

TEODORA

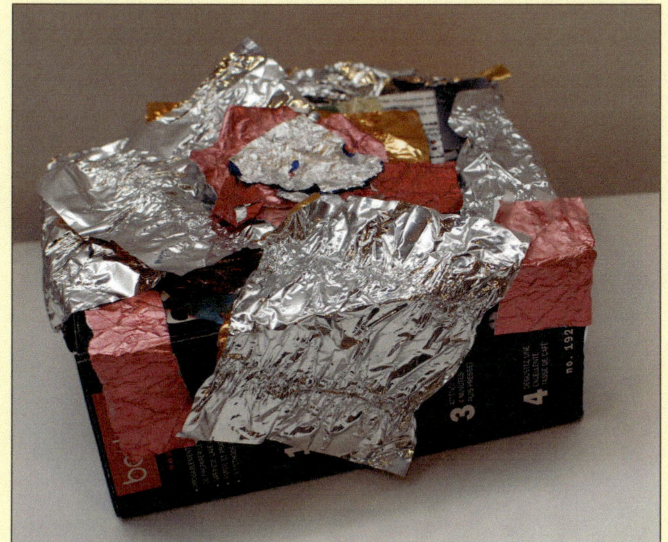

ABOUT THE ARTIST

Teodora is always ready to go to the art studio, whether on her own or with friends. She enjoys many different materials, though showing a preference for collage with shiny papers and watercolor painting. An independent artist, Tea likes to make her own choices regarding materials ("I choose!"), and she makes it a point to get those materials on her own, even if it involves struggling with tricky drawers or high shelves. When something does not quite meet her expectations, Teodora finds her way around it: "Maybe later. Maybe next time."

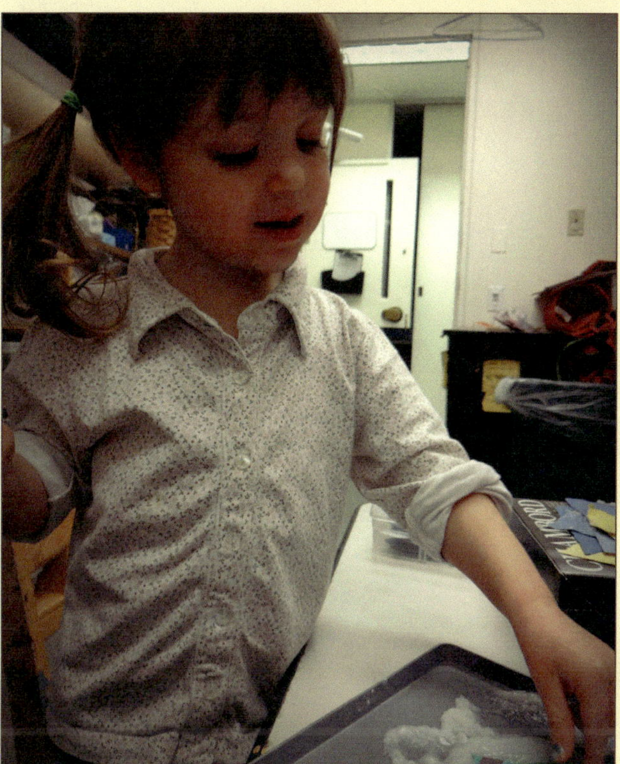

IN HER OWN WORDS

I like to build.

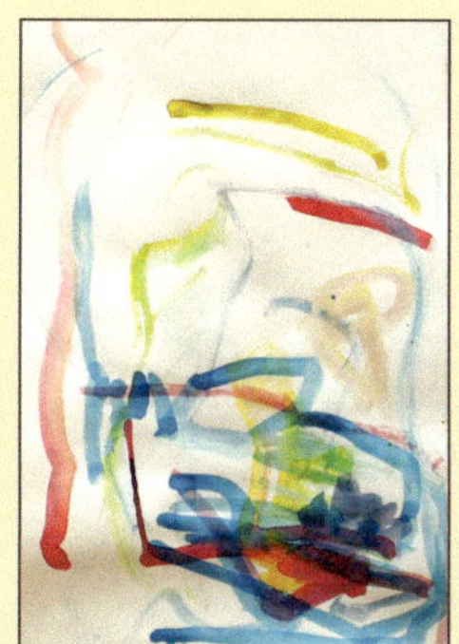

Monkey bars.

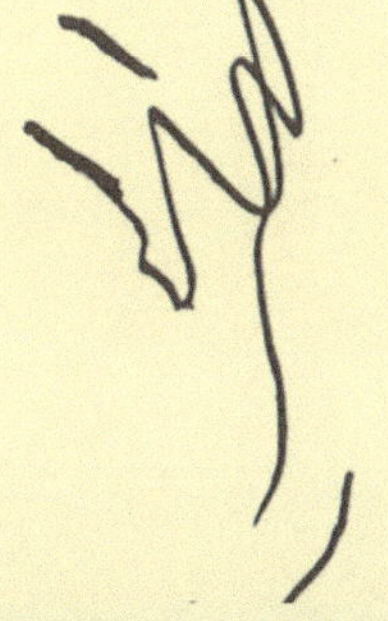

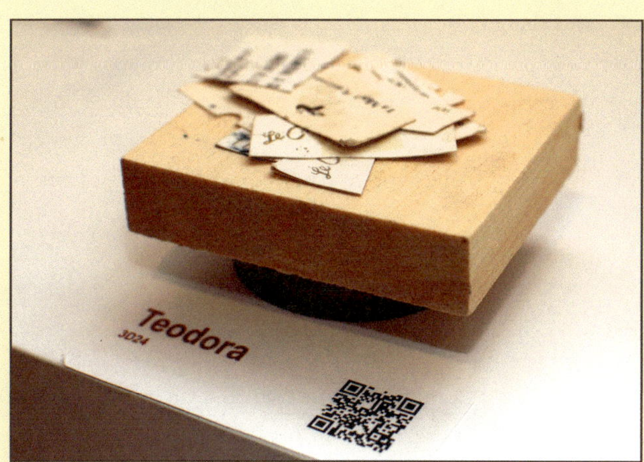

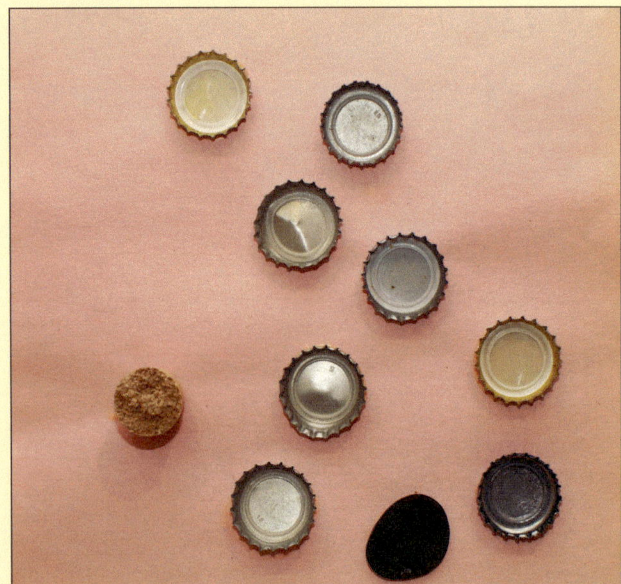

The lizard is hiding. I made it. I glued the lizard.

ABOUT THE ARTIST

In her quest for discovery of the possibilities different materials have to offer, Zaria often enjoys getting messy, and likes reassurance that it is okay to do so. Sometimes, when experiences may be too much to take in all at once, Zaria takes a moment to step back and observe, returning to her hands-on explorations and sharing her insights a few minutes later. Zaria particularly enjoys painting, collage, and clay. She likes to work both with tools and with her hands, and enjoys looking around for new materials with which to work. Zaria likes to work in the art studio and often talks about what she is experiencing, making sure her friends and teacher are listening.

IN HER OWN WORDS

I like to paint with pink. Just pink. And, I like purple. I'm 3 [pointing to the number three written on the date (2013) on her painting]. I like these paints.

ZARIA

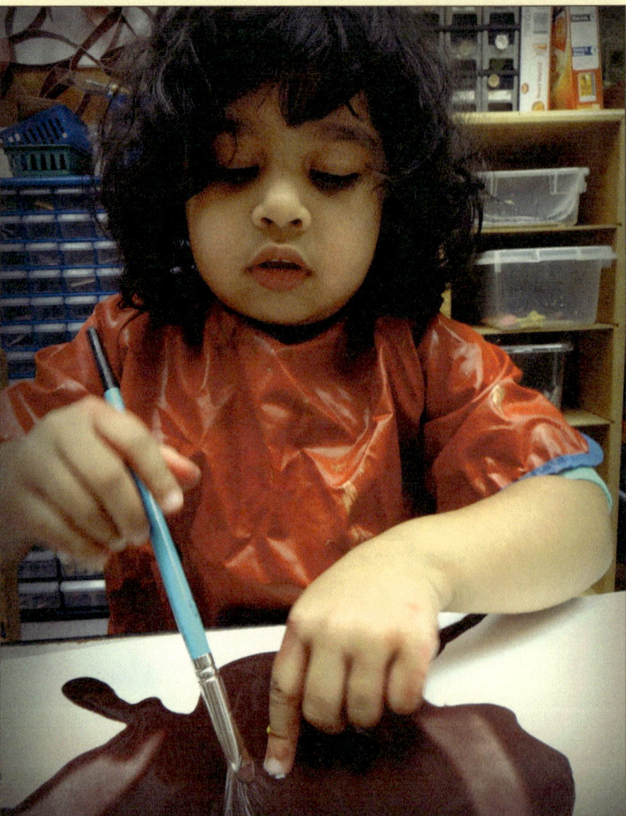

I used this one, and this one, and this one. Boxes. Hari and Zaria used glue. It's a plane! It's just like an airplane! I wanna show it to Mommy and Daddy. Because we're flying. Flying in a plane, to the city.

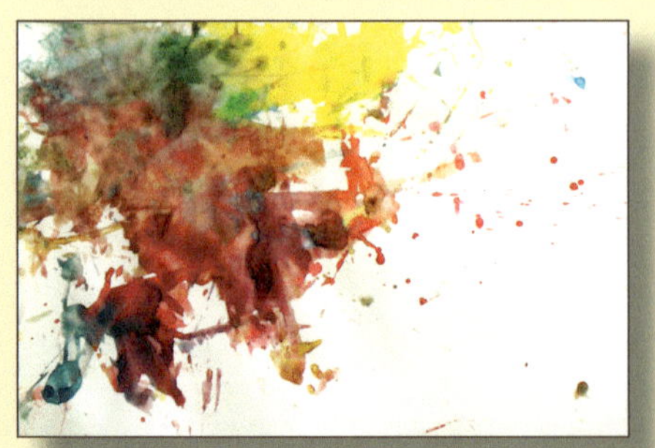

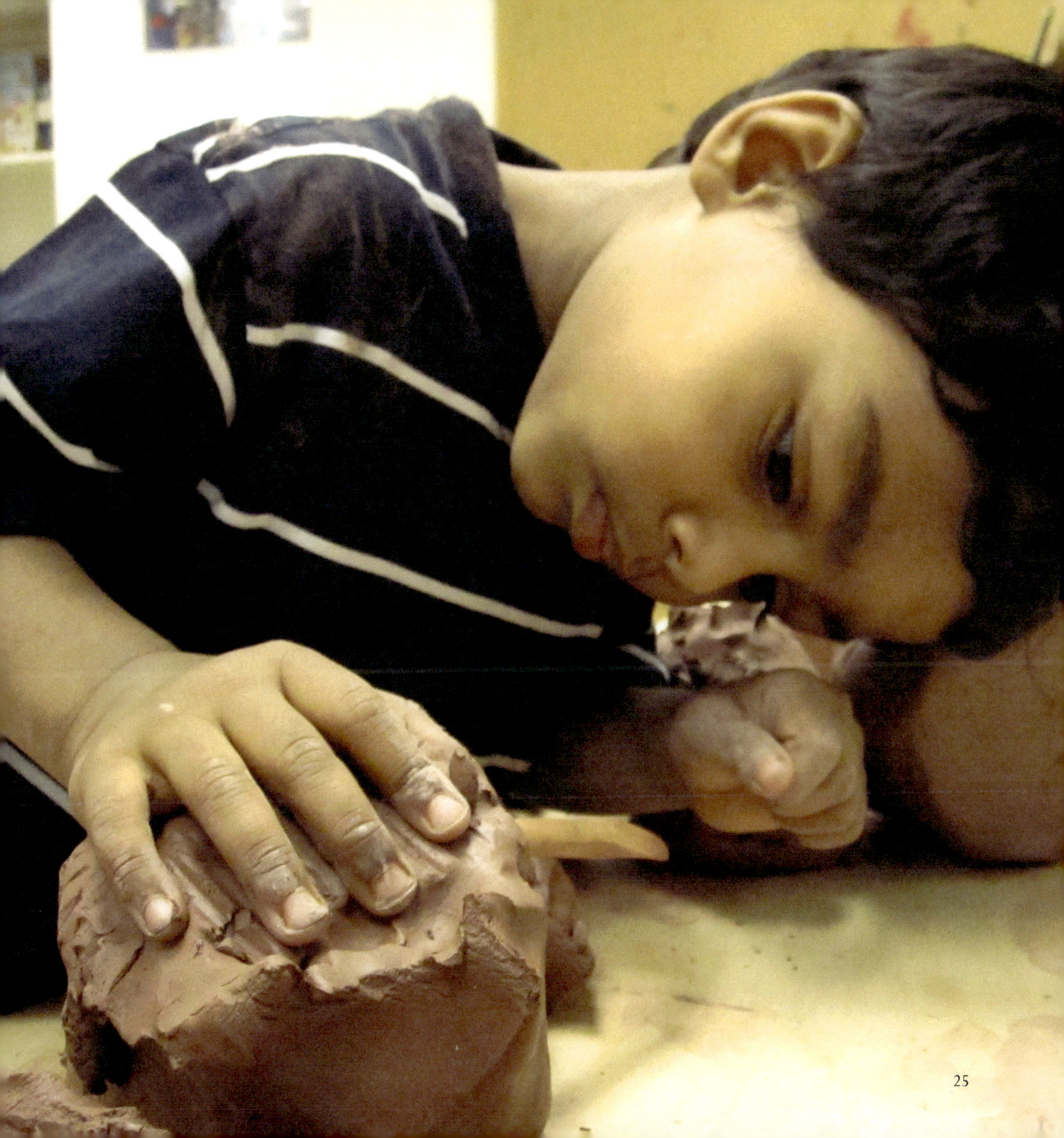

CURATORS, ARTISTS & TOUR GUIDES: SETTING UP & RUNNING THE ART EXHIBITION

"Where's my work? Where's my work? There's my work!" Teodora skips and hops into the gallery ahead of everyone else, racing for the spot where she placed her poster, and looking to find the 3D pieces she selected to show.

Like most other toddlers and preschoolers, Teodora is well aware of which pieces of hers are on display, where in the gallery they are located, and even what the QR codes next to them refer to. She, like the other children, played a significant role in setting up the show, and is well aware of many of the numerous steps that the long preparation for this exhibition entailed.

This exhibition begins and ends with the children and their artistic explorations, and the children are actively engaged in the process of making it happen. They do this work with the master-curator[1], who develops and curates the exhibition as such, but who does not determine each artist's individual choices. I see my work in this show as an effort "to bring a selection of […] works of art, into a shared space […] with the aim of demonstrating, primarily through the experiential accumulation of visual connections, a particular constellation of meanings that cannot be made known by any other means"[2]. As the master-curator, my work goes towards designing those constellations in a way that showcases the artworks not only as stand-alone products but also

as representative of the ways in which I see the children's processes throughout the school year, of their ideas, and of themselves as artistic explorers of materials.

As we start preparing for the exhibition, children are invited to select which pieces to show. However, this decision making process is not the same for all children. Whereas some toddlers and preschoolers have a clear idea in their minds about which artworks they want to exhibit or are happy to go through all their artworks to make their selection, other children have worked on so many pieces that the choice could become overwhelming. Being so, the way children participate in choosing depends on their ways of learning and being. It is up to the teacher to find ways that best suit each child.

When children have a large body of work, I may pre-select a few pieces for them to choose from, making it more manageable. However, the way I make this pre-selection is based on the experiences I have seen the children engage with each work, as well as taking into consideration how they may, on the one hand, better represent their exploratory process and, on the other, fit within the general constellation of the exhibition. This is also what happens with some of the youngest children, who may be prolific painters but eventually have a harder time choosing between a

---

1   Cooper, M., & Sjostrom, L. (2006). *Making art together. how collaborative art-making can transform kids, classrooms, and communities*. Boston, MA: Beacon Press.

2   Smith, T. (2012, p. 30.). *Thinking contemporary curating*. New York, NY: Independent Curators International.

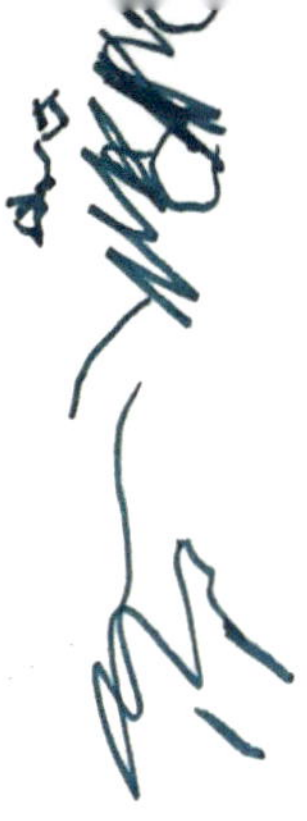

large array of works. Infants, for example, participate in this decision-making process in many ways: the selected works may be the ones they crawl to, grab, or mouth, when all the pieces are laid out on the floor in front of them. Other times, young children make their choices very clear to the teachers, as Callie does when she decisively tosses some of her paintings (or rips parts of her paintings) on the floor, seemingly refusing to take them back if they're handed back to her.

Along with the selection of the pieces, the children and I work on artist statements and short artist bios. Each child shares she or he wants the exhibition's visitors to know about themselves as artists, and talk about their work and their explorations. Before the pieces are ready to be installed in the gallery, these statements and bios are read back to the children for a final check, and it is not that unusual that a change of heart, a life event, or a misunderstood word eventually leads to revisions and new edits. That was the case when Carter and his older sister Carmela were revising his artist statement in which he mentioned Tuesday, his cat.

As I read the statement back to him, Carter announced that Tuesday had died that week, and we talked about missing and remembering our loved ones. Carter and Carmela together decided that Tuesday was still very present in their lives and should remain present in the art show too - and so they chose to add a note about Tuesday to Carter's original statement, making Carter's work more deeply related to his own lived and meaningful experiences.

As the pieces and statements are ready, it is time to finally install the exhibition in the gallery. As in many art exhibitions, many of the curatorial efforts here go into displaying the artwork in ways that allow pieces to "play together" and shine both as individual works and as part of an ensemble of works, representing each artist while being part of an exhibition with its own coherence and identity.

As such, the artworks selected by the children are then carefully organized in the gallery, but the process of actually putting them up on the walls is each artist's task: in small groups, the children go up to the gallery, do one final check of their work while it lies on the floor, and go about installing it by pasting mounting squares (or "really sticky square stickers," as Haram described them) to the back of their posters, peeling the protective layer off, and sticking the works to the wall making sure they go just above the line of blue tape.

The blue tape line - painters tape - is placed in advance as an even line across the gallery, so that the children (or whoever is installing) know the exact height that their works should be hung. As an object, it allows the children to be autonomous and to help each other in the the process of installing this exhibition, once all the pieces are up and the blue line is no longer needed, peeling it off the wall is also a fun part of the process, and many children enjoy pulling and playing with the tape in inventive ways like William did when wrapping himself up in tape as "Blue Tape Man Superhero."

In the installation and throughout the duration of the exhibition, many are the ways in which toddlers and preschoolers are actively involved in running and interacting with it. These ways seem to reinforce their sense of ownership over, as well as their role in, the exhibit. Leading guided tours is one of these ways; on a daily basis during the exhibition, children walk visitors through the show, talking about the artworks, their processes of exploring materials, and taking questions and comments - or sometimes crawling and meowing like cats through it all, like Clara and Zaria often enjoyed doing.

In these tours, children talk about their own artworks and also other pieces in the gallery, interpreting and making connections between what they experience in the gallery, their experiences with materials, and their daily interactions with their peers.

But toddlers and preschoolers are busy people and, according to Haram, "don't have much time." There's playing, and napping, and going to the park, and kids can't always be in the gallery to welcome visitors. So how can we still have visitors engaging not only with the artworks but with children's thoughts and stories as well? How can I, the master-curator, offer insights to children's statements without being overly didactic and overshadowing the artworks?

How can I create places and spaces for the children's voices and narratives without cluttering the exhibition and taking away its identity as an art exhibition?

The solution for this year's *Broken Things Can Be Beautiful Things* exhibition was QR codes, small square codes that, when scanned with a smartphone or other device, led directly to each child's artist statement about each piece, either in audio form or as a written text. In this way the exhibition remained clean and uncluttered, with a small amount of text on each label so as not to distract viewers from the pieces themselves, but at the same time, the codes allowed for a large amount of information to be conveyed directly from the children.

Although QR codes are widely used in many settings, for some visitors it was a new experience. Unfamiliar with such technology and unsure of how to deal with it, many visitors relied on the children to tell them what to do and what those little squares were. "This one is for Constantin's work," Uma explained as she pointed to the QR code next to her friend's piece, "and this one is my Dog River sculpture. It's my artist statement."

For many parents, this exhibition was a first encounter with the QR code technology, and scanning their child's work code became a window into a new way of interacting not only with this show but with this technology in general. "We scanned our first QR code to find 'Apple!, Apple!'," Liam's mom said as she read her child's artist statement on her phone. For some visitors, it was surprising to find such a technology in an exhibition of young artists. It may be making a statement that an exhibition of very young children's art was the first one at Macy Gallery to use this technology as an integral part of its curatorial process, as it provided the show with an increased sense of seriousness and professionalism not always associated with children's art.

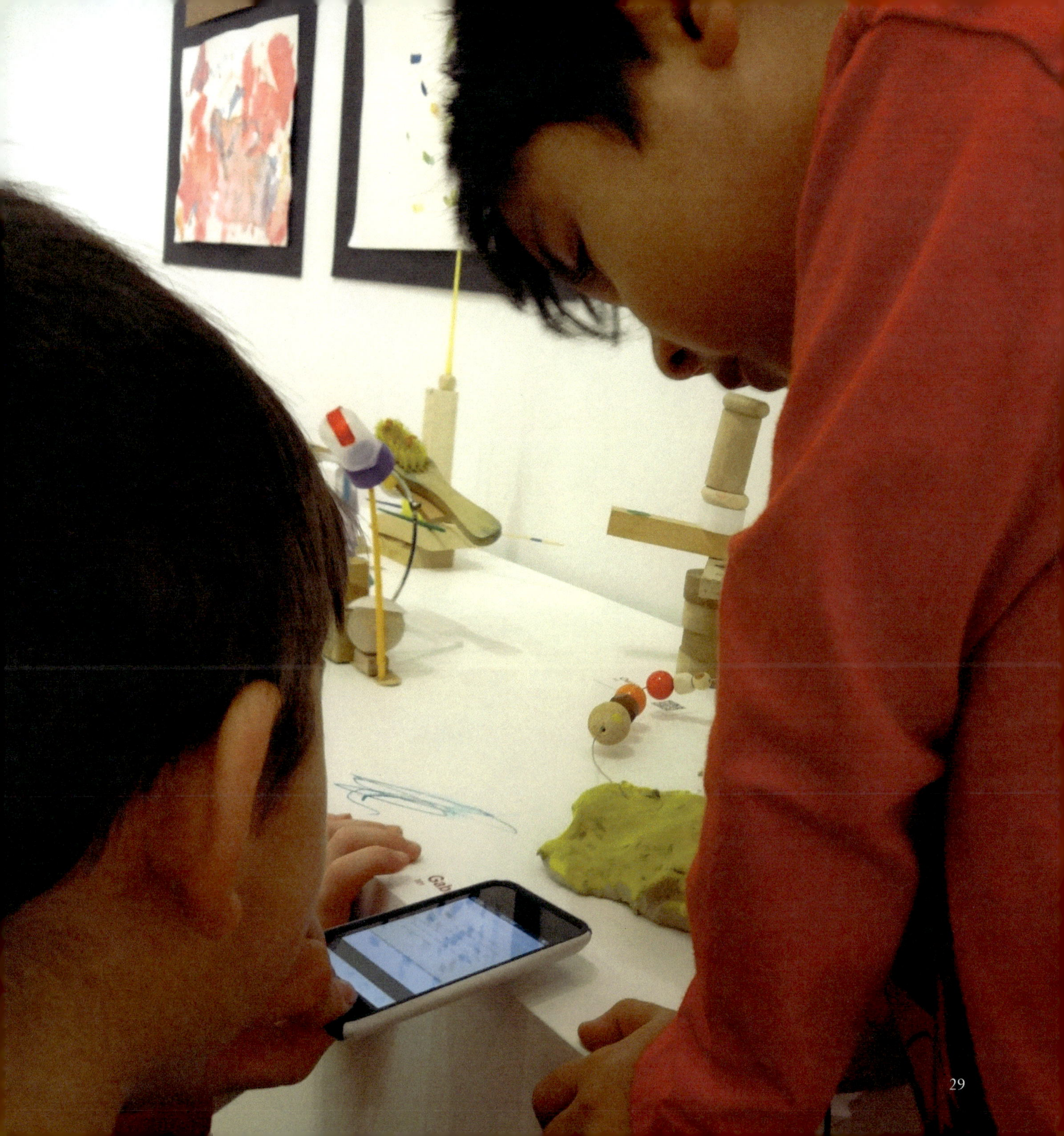

PRESCHOOLERS

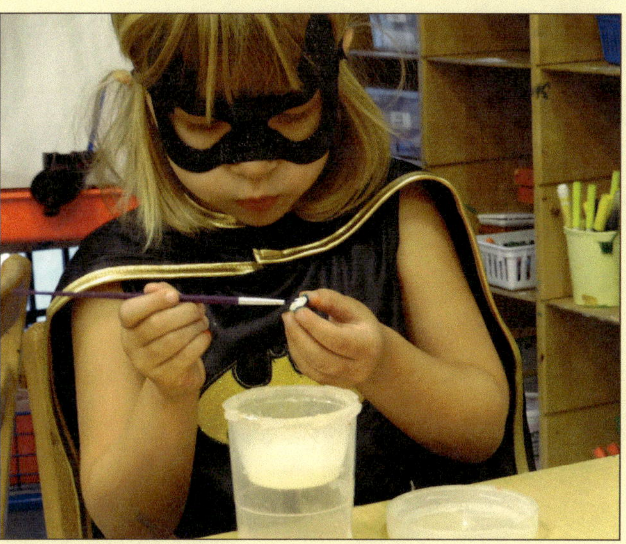

I am very proud of myself. Because I did a really good job.

ABOUT THE ARTIST

Annabelle creates art with joy and enthusiasm. She likes patterns and sequences, and carefully keeps her work and workspace tidy and organized. Annabelle pays meticulous attention to details in her own artwork and in the artwork of others and likes to share what she notices. Sometimes she clarifies what specific elements mean to her, as she did while looking at William's artwork: "I like that it has many things on it. And of course I like the heart. It means 'I love you'."

Conversations often inspire Annabelle to add more details to her work. She enjoys making art to offer her mommy or her friends, and she often includes specific elements that she believes each specific person will appreciate.

IN HER OWN WORDS

I live at the preschool room. I am 4 ½. I like to make rainbow art. A rainbow is when you put colors in the sky, but it's on art, so it's not in the sky. All the colors here make it rainbowy because rainbows have a lot of colors. I like to do all of each art as possible. Sometimes I like to work with my friends, and sometimes I like to work on my own. You can hold your hand up and paint whatever you want. You go water, sponge, paper with your brush.

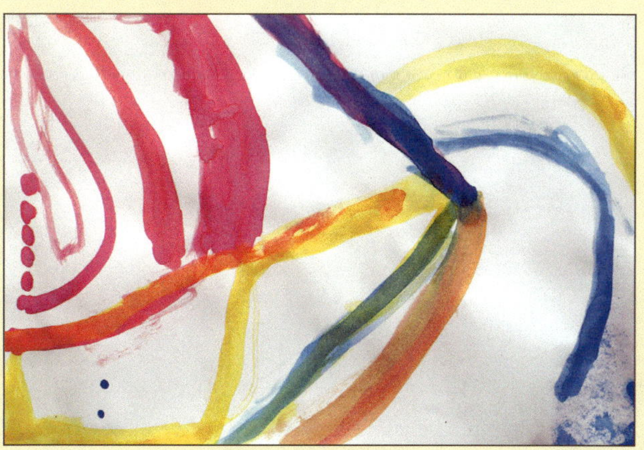

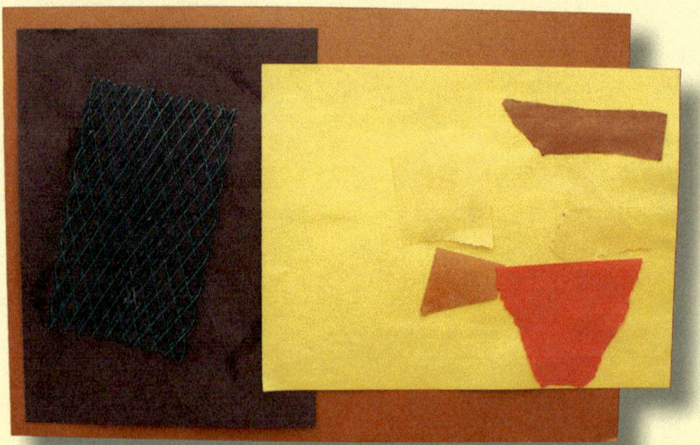

I remember this one. I put only one thing there. I choose this work because it looks so cute. Because this is actually me. Because this is my tummy and I wanted to show my tummy in the art show. Nothing else, I will only show my tummy.

ABOUT THE ARTIST

Carter's family often serves as inspiration for his artwork, as in the case of the collage he chose to exhibit here, representing Mommy, Daddy, Carmela, and Tuesday. Carter enjoys exploring different materials and tools, and especially likes the texture of clay.

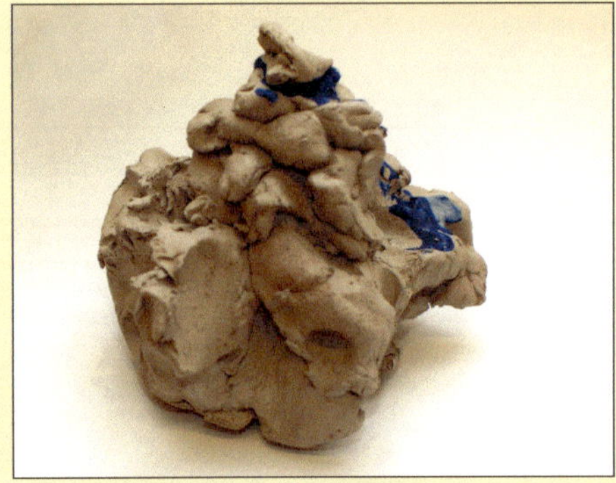

I put paint on it and nothing else. It looks like a statue. Actually it looks like Ariel. I used tools. Sharp tools.

CARTER

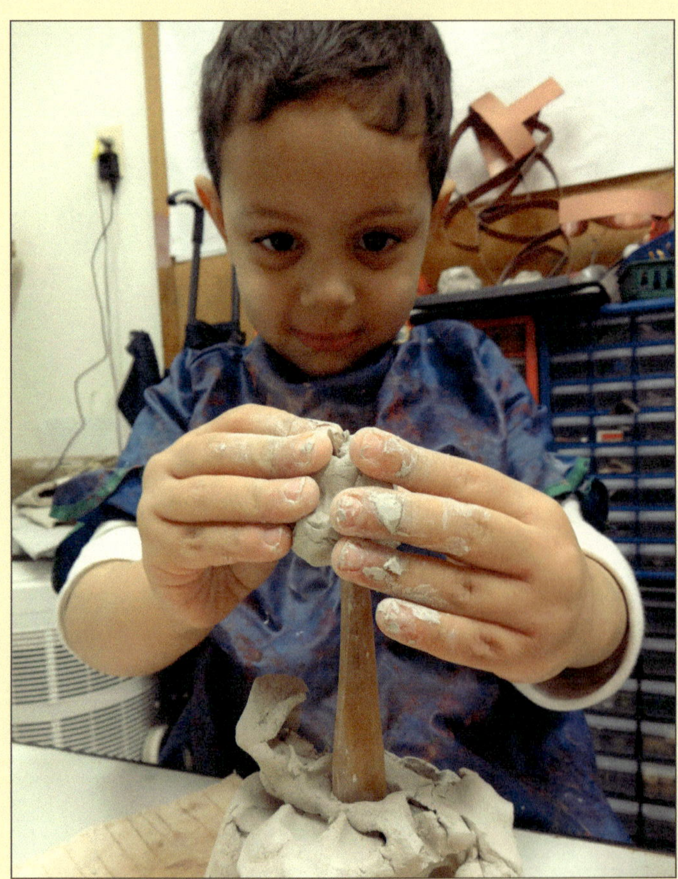

IN HIS OWN WORDS

I like to play with clay. Because it's mushy clay. I like to paint. I like to make art with other friends. Tuesday [Carter's cat] is not coming to the art show because cats can't come to school. At home I can just tell him about it because he listens to people talking to him. I can talk in cat language. Blue is my favorite color.
[Carmela added: Tuesday died on February 17th, 2014. He was sick.]

CONSTANTIN

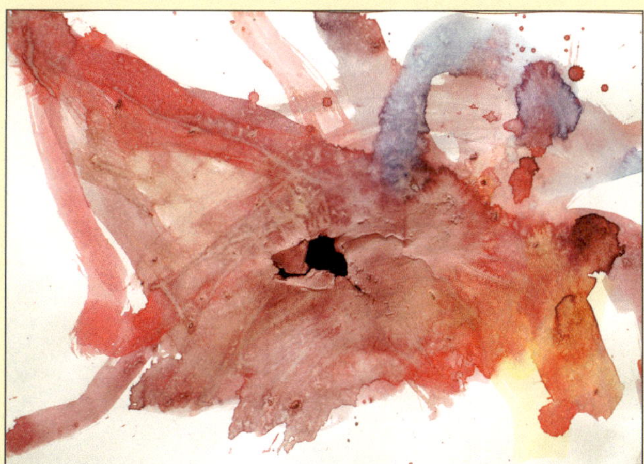

It's broken. I broken it. I need a new paper. I need clean water.

ABOUT THE ARTIST

Constantin uses his full body to engage with materials. He becomes fully immersed in his artistic explorations, particularly with 3D materials like clay, which he enjoys squishing and poking. Constantin creates elaborate forms with his clay, using different actions to change its shape over and over again, responding to the prompts he gets from the material. He often uses toys and other tools to play with materials.

Play is an integral part of his art, and when he goes to the art studio, Constantin is usually on his way to scare monsters away ("Get away, monsters!"), or some other equally animated enterprise.

IN HIS OWN WORDS

I like the clay. I like the fork (tool). Soft. Me, I'm the biggest.

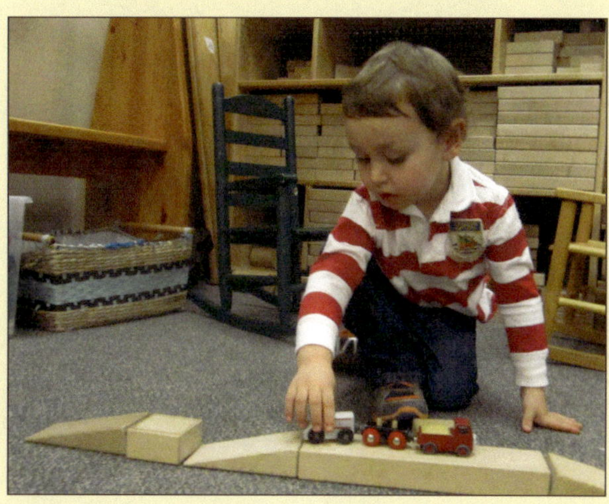

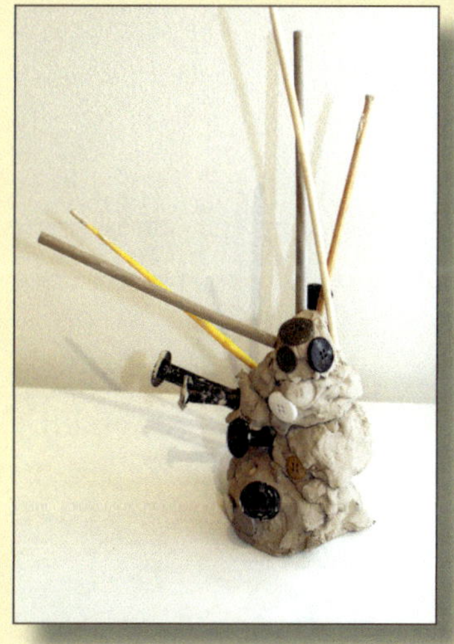

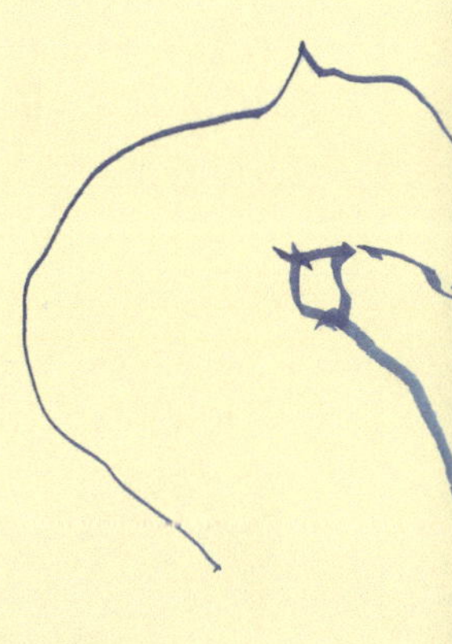

Look, Marta, look! I broke. I broke, I used the cuteau. This is a château. I live in the château with Dylan! My bed is there, and Daddy's is there, and Mommy there! Watch me. I'm making a tiger too. I'm making a lion. A light. I'm making a tree. Look, haha! Look, two yellow lights. Look, this is my castle! This is Dylan, this is me! Look, this is my doggie!

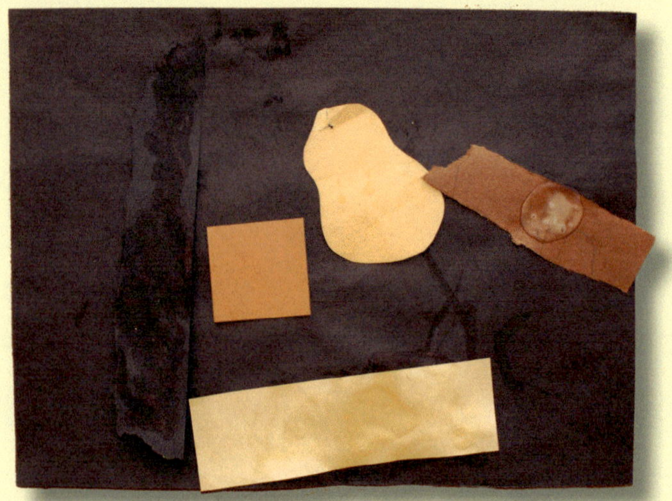

DYLAN

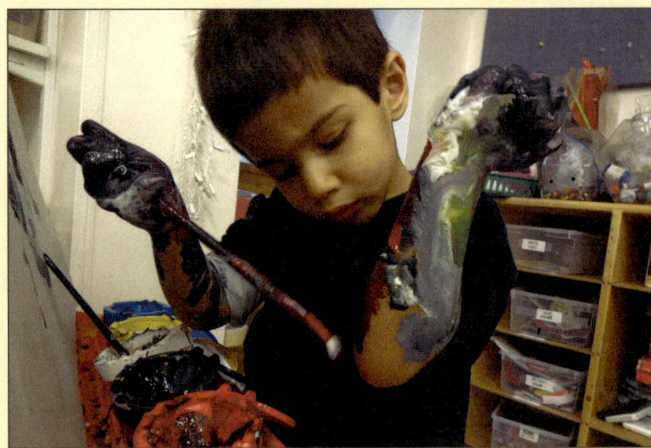

ABOUT THE ARTIST

An enthusiastic artist with a particular interest in investigating properties and possibilities of clay, Dylan is resolute in stating his plans for his day in the art studio. "I want art. I want clay," he states firmly. When getting his clay and tools, Dylan lets his teachers know what he needs: "I want to play with the big one. This – this is the big one." Dylan enjoys playing with the clay tools and is happy to put his clay back into a ball when he is done, saving it to be used another time. He likes to have the company of his teacher as he explores materials, calling attention to his discoveries: *Look, Marta, look! Look what I'm doing!*

IN HIS OWN WORDS

When selecting this particular collage to show in the exhibition, Dylan recalled his process: "I like to put this on there."

Describing his watercolor process during one classroom meeting, Dylan tells his friends and teachers "I painted. I just went to the art studio with my friend."

As he was working on his sculpture, Dylan studied different ways of including all the desired elements, moving the bottle caps around to make space for the paper as well. He ended up gluing caps on top of paper, describing his technique of gluing the caps down onto the wood: "And tap, tap, tap it! Like the paper!"

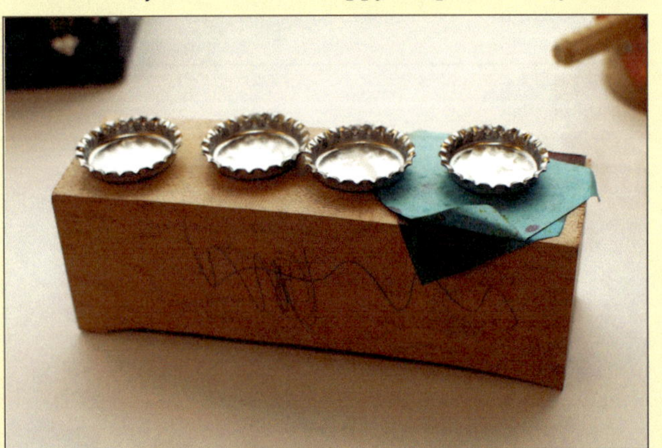

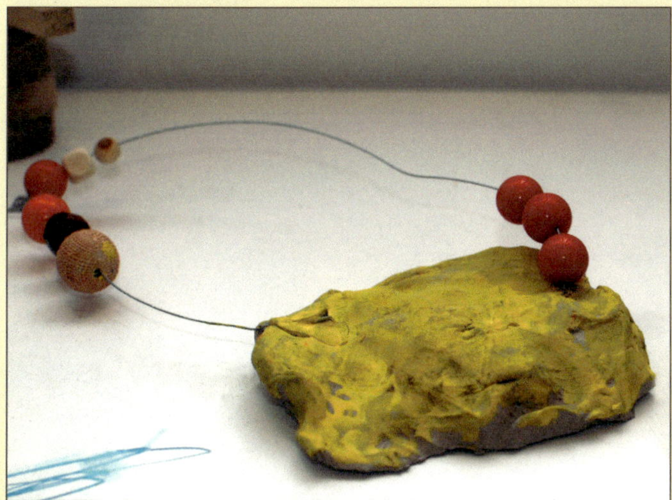

I paint like this because, if a bad guy walks, they slip and they have yellow faces and they get smushed. It's a trap. Under here, a gun pokes out and shoots the bad guys. The gun is made of wood.

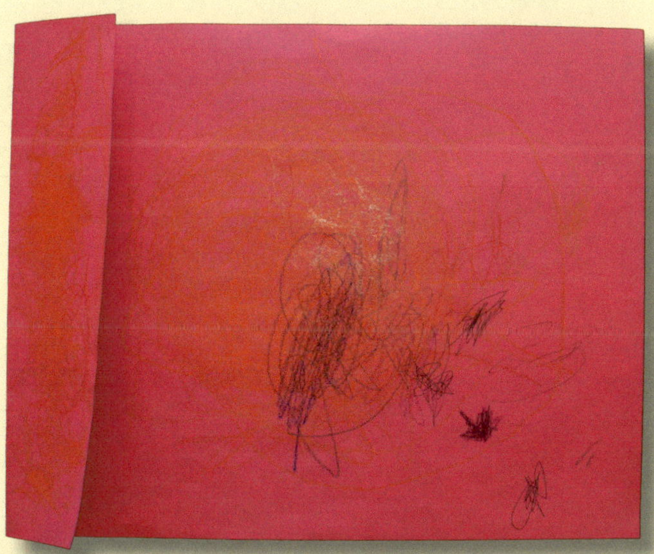

How did I make it? I went crazy. All around here and all around here. He flies, but not very well.

GABRIEL

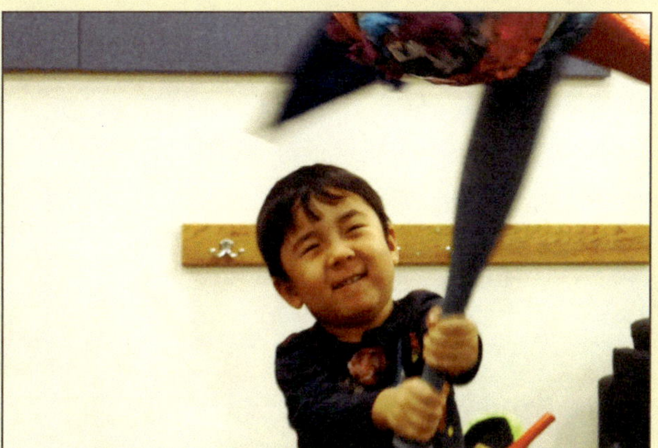

ABOUT THE ARTIST

Gabriel creates many narratives to go along with his explorations of materials, and likes telling his stories to his friends and teachers. He often shares his expertise in color mixing with his friends, both explaining what he is working on, and giving advice as to how to mix one color or another: "This is orange, look! I mixed red and yellow and I got orange and I made it look kind of like purple."

Gabriel often works on self-portraits and represents himself along with his friends and superhero companions: "This is my ear yellow. Then my face will be red. Haram, that's me and then I'll draw you, okay? There, that's you!"

IN HIS OWN WORDS

I'm 3. I want to be Tonistre instead of Gabriel. No, Gabriel! In the art studio I like to sit on a chair, look at things.

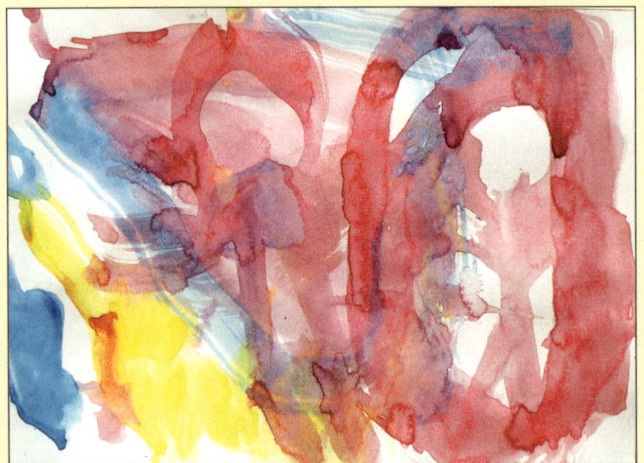

HARAM

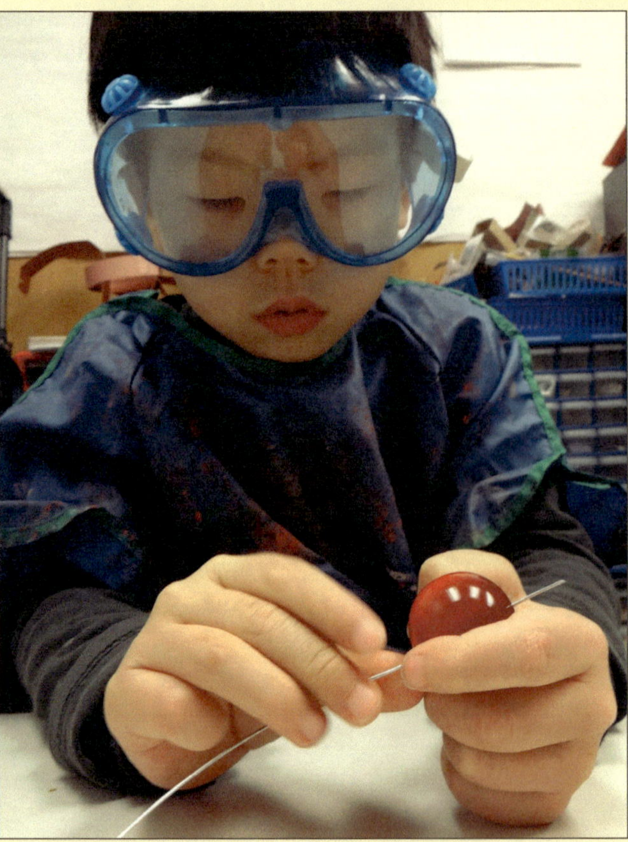

ABOUT THE ARTIST

When Haram is waiting for an artwork to dry up, he is vigilant – making sure whoever worked with him is equally so. He keeps track of where and in which condition his artworks are, talking about his experiences with enthusiasm. Haram enjoys working with paint and with clay, and revisits his own narratives about himself and his fellow superheroes in many of his watercolors. If the materials behave in unexpected ways, Haram is quick to adapt his narratives to what he is experiencing, and he explores alternative ways of telling his stories. He likes to explore the possibilities of different tools, and often in his watercolors, investigates the ways in which different brushes make different marks.

IN HIS OWN WORDS

Look what the fan brush can do! This brush can also do zigzag. I like that my brush is camouflage, you cannot see it! [The brush is fully dipped in the paint]. If you want to put it [the clay] down, you have to flatten it like this [pounding]. This looks like a little fish. Swim, little fish! How can art not get any dirt?! Silly!

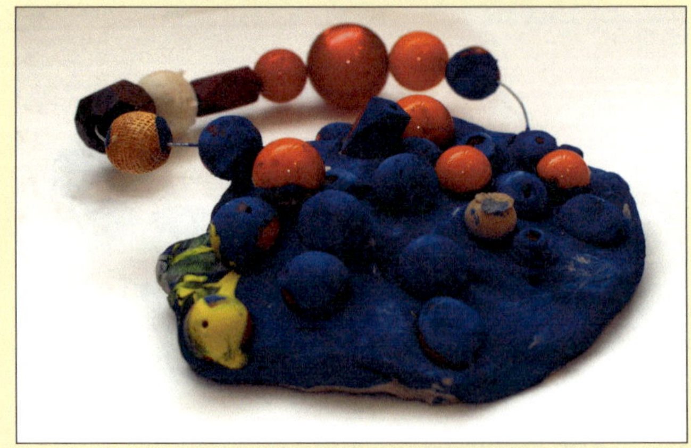

ABOUT THE ARTIST

Kinley enjoys exploring materials and the possibilities they offer, often finding innovative solutions like she did while working with paint on a large piece of paper.

Kinley enjoys the quietness of the art studio and often uses it as a transition space as she gets to school. She likes to collaborate with her mother when working in the classroom some mornings, as she explains with this particular watercolor:

KINLEY

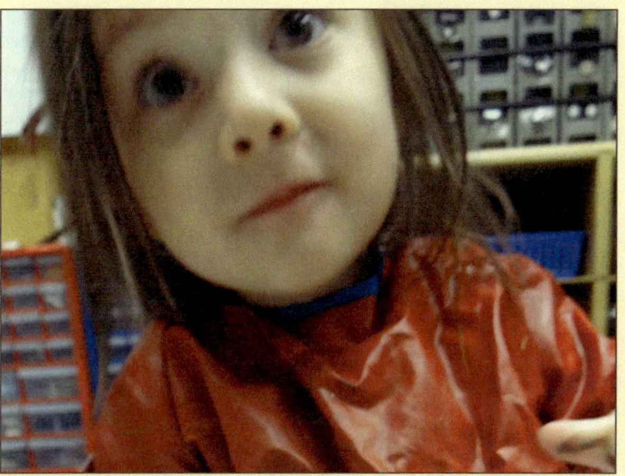

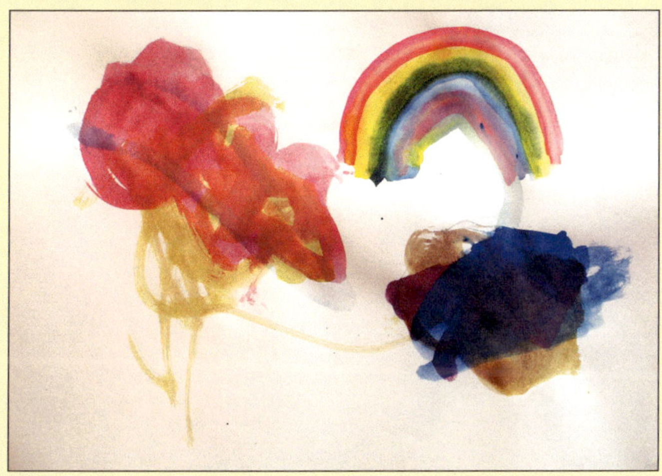

This is my painting. Mommy made the rainbow.

IN HER OWN WORDS

I'm Kinley. I'm Colten's sister. I'm 3.

While exploring her clay, Kinley shared her thoughts: "I'm making a hole. I can make it bigger. I feel something there. There's more clay inside the clay. I feel it. It feels wet. I'm putting this piece inside that hole. I took some clay out. It feels messy. I need more tools."

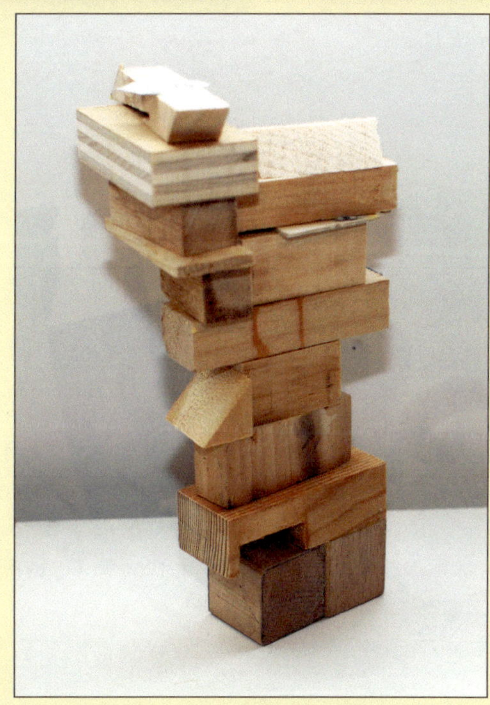

I'm making a big castle. It's a big house. Now I'm gonna use some ribbon. I'm gonna make this into a surprise for my mommy's birthday.

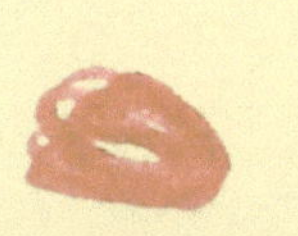

LEAH

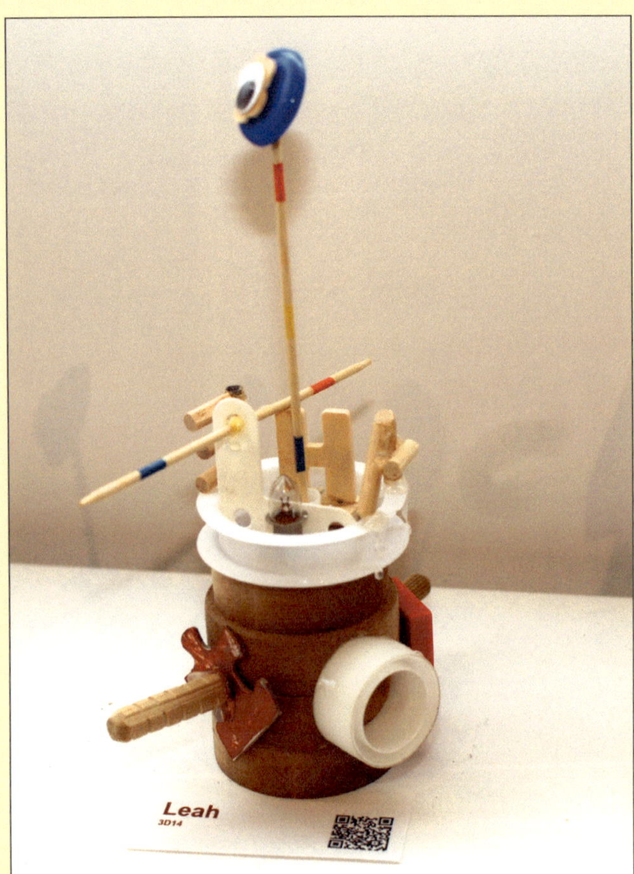

Leah
3D14

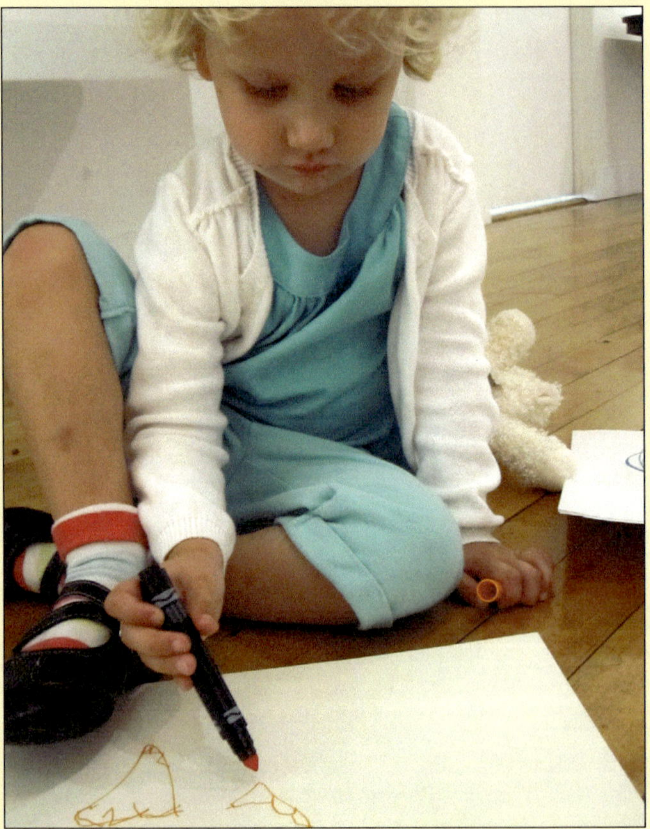

ABOUT THE ARTIST

Leah pays great attention to detail in her artistic explorations, both while making and talking about her works. She enjoys experimenting with different materials and finds various uses for her tools and materials to serve her interests and purposes.

IN HER OWN WORDS

I like using scissors. I'm 3 ½. I like to draw on my own. My favorite colors are pink and purple. I like making sculptures. I like to use things that I find for my sculptures.

I used scissors. I cut. It's a diamond. It opens.

OWEN

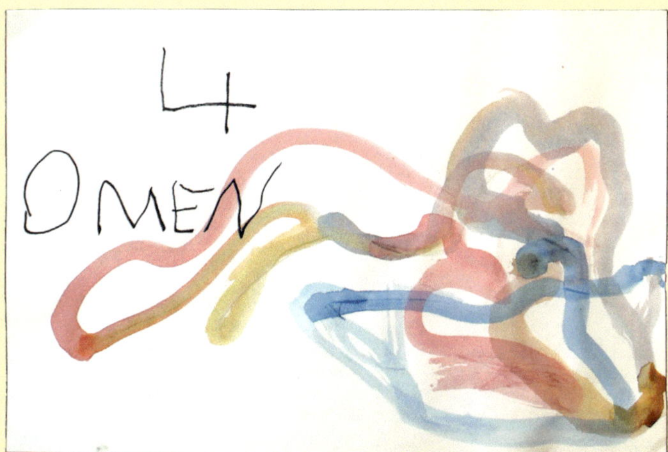

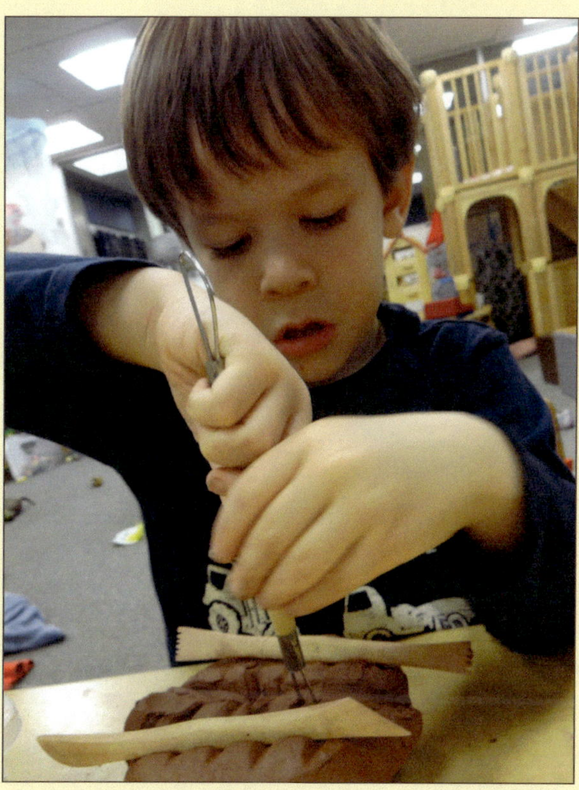

ABOUT THE ARTIST

Owen's interests inform his artistic explorations, and he often narrates his experiences with materials using dinosaurs, football, or other stories, as he did when he narrated his clay play, poking holes and covering them up: "I'm a paleontologist working with these tools! I'm making a cave. An animal is going in the cave. I'm covering all the caves." Owen likes to use tools to change the materials he has at hand. He uses different tools for different purposes, and when toys are included, they are usually used as mark-making tools as well.

IN HIS OWN WORDS

My favorite color is pink, and red can make pink by adding white. I'm 4. Sometimes I like mixing colors. I like to make paintings, build sculptures. I like to work in the preschool room and at home, on my own. I like to look at other people's art. My favorite color used to be blue, but now it's pink.

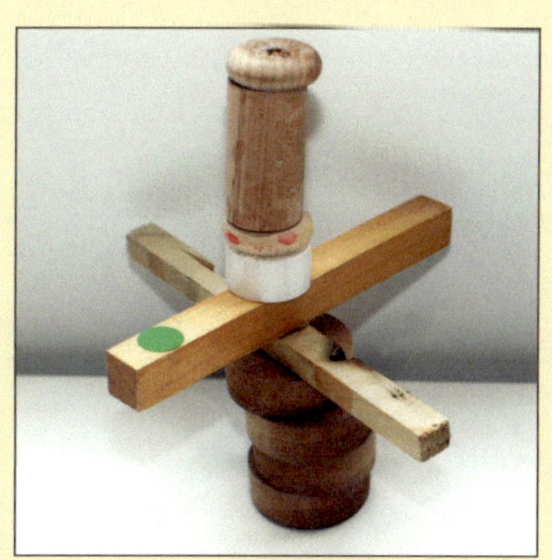

PACO

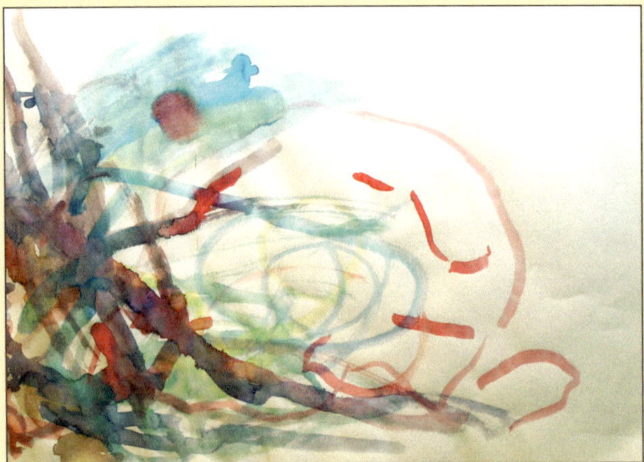

I choose this one because it's make fast.

ABOUT THE ARTIST

An attentive artist, Paco is interested in different media and notices different things about each material, verbalizing as he goes. He often talks about shapes, textures, and sizes when looking at artworks or art materials, and the properties of materials inspire him to push the boundaries of traditional approaches ("…the glue it's on my finger! I could stick my finger in the collage!") and to find solutions for in his explorations ("It's gonna be like that because the small one I can't fit. You see"). As he works, Paco often describes his processes: "Look, I'm trying to get all my clay out. I swiped it on the table, and then wipe with the sponge and then the clay is on the sponge. It's all brown. Now I squishing it and the clay goes out. Now my hands are all clay."

IN HIS OWN WORDS

Art is when we paint. I like watercolor paints because there's three colors and I like to do lines. Yellow is my favorite color. I like to mix it with other colors. I'm almost 4. I like to make sculptures with racecars. I like to go to the gallery and see art.

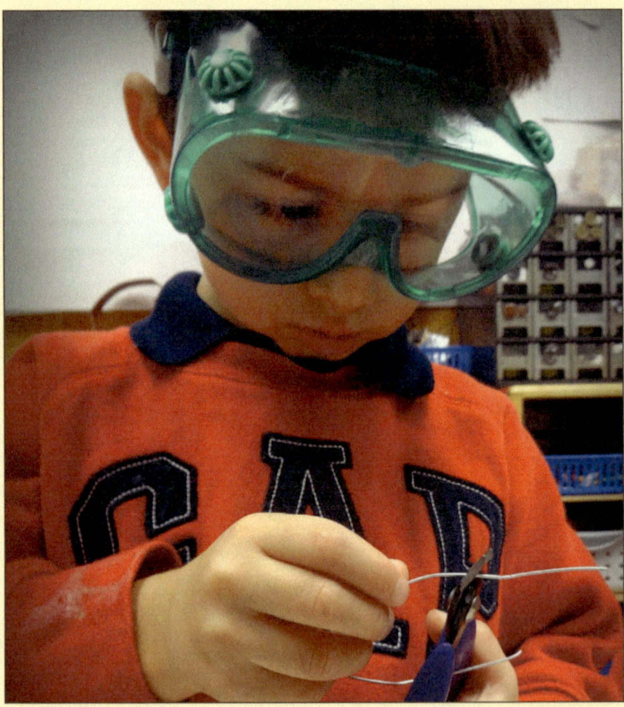

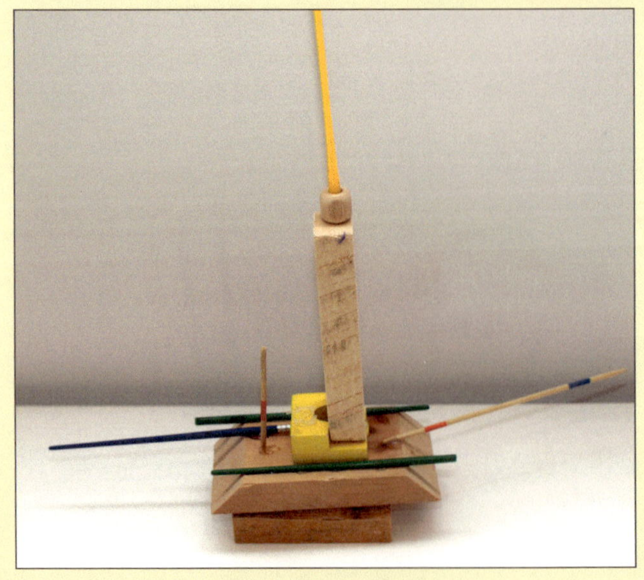

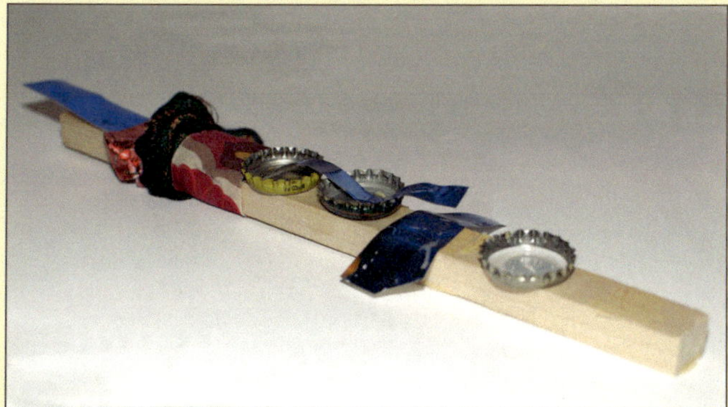

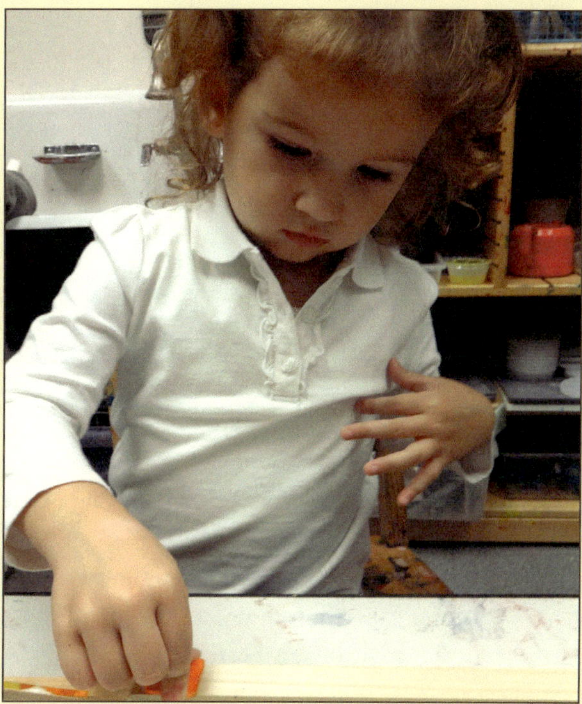

SOFIA

ABOUT THE ARTIST

Sofia is an enthusiastic artist, verbal in her explorations. As she works, she questions the possibilities of the materials and finds solutions by experimenting in different ways. "How can I glue this paper on top?", she asks herself. Sofia observes the results of every action she makes. Materials, such as the sparkly chocolate wrap, also inspire her sculpture: "I want to make this sparkly!" In a classroom meeting, she explained to her friends and teachers what she was up to that morning: "I was arting. I was working with construction that we built, and that's how I made my sparkly airplane flower."

IN HER OWN WORDS

If I have the most beautifulest art then I can be the winner. But there's no winner. Then we can just choose to get some art because there is not very much space. I'm 3 1/2. I like to do cool art. It's some art that has a lot of things on top. With clay and with wood. Sometimes I use tools, and then when I make a wing, sometimes I make a plane. My favorite art is sparkly airplane flower. Another artist told me how to be an artist. It was an idea in my head, it was not a real story. It's fun to see other people's art because I like to see it. I like to talk about it and I like to see all the different things. All the cool things. I thinks it's going to be really, really awesome to see that, that I can see somebody else's art.

I found all these sparkly papers to make my construction beautiful. I used all of these papers to make it shiny. It looks very sparkly like my favorite flowers. Sparkly flowers. It's made of wood and blue thing, and red sparkly paper and this thing I don't know how it's called. This is a top of a thing that you pull water and another one and this is another blue thing and this is another top thing that you pull water or wine. It was broken before and I made art. But these tops are not broken. I like to make art with broken things and I also painted it. I like the broken things because I'll make it really cool.

SOPHIA

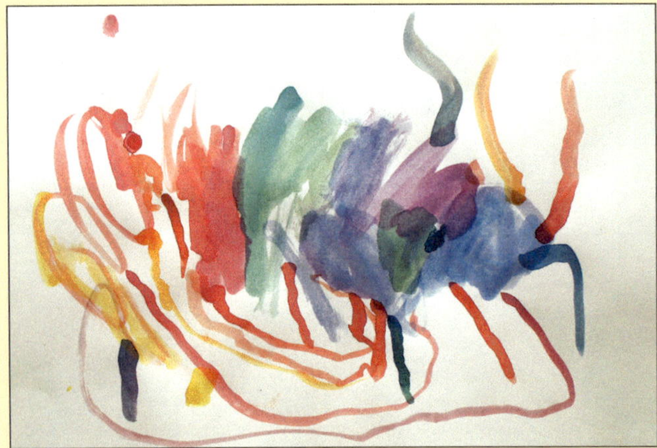

ABOUT THE ARTIST

Sophia is an avid explorer of materials and enjoys experimenting with different techniques. She is methodical in the way she tries out her tools, and likes to share her discoveries with her friends and teachers: "Whenever time I'm doing this, I make a bigger hole. I'm twisting the tool. It gets bigger." She often recalls previous times she worked with the same materials, bringing back the narratives she created and the discoveries she made about the materials, but all within reason according to what she knows about the world — "Pink can't talk," she explains. When asked if her lines are friends with each other, she quips, "Only in your imagination".

IN HER OWN WORDS

I'm 4. Big people are not 4. Pink and purple and yellow are my favorite colors. I like sculpture art because of how it stands. I like to use soft and rough materials. I like to make sculptures with broken things because broken things can be nice things.

Broken things make nice things. Broken things. You need to think about what to do with broken things.

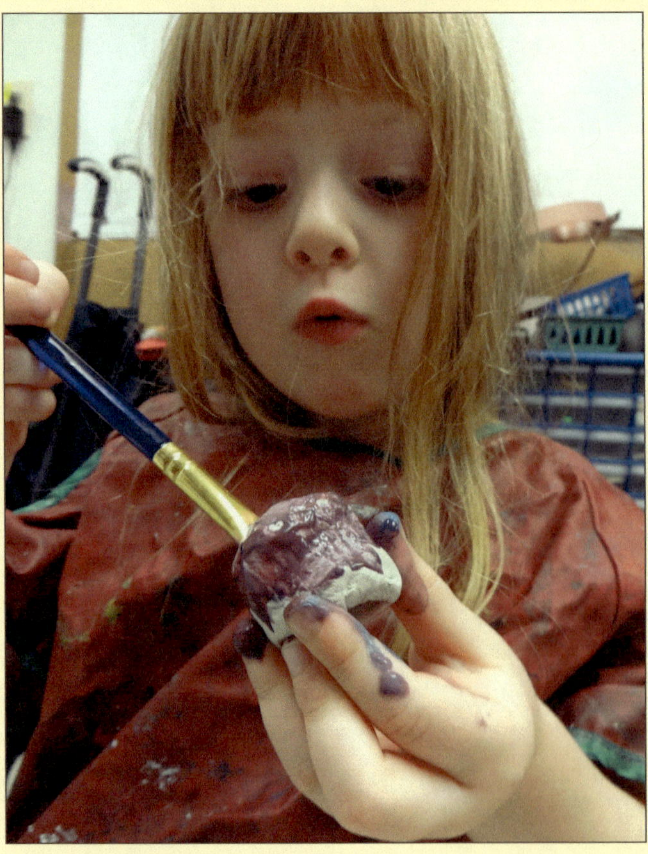

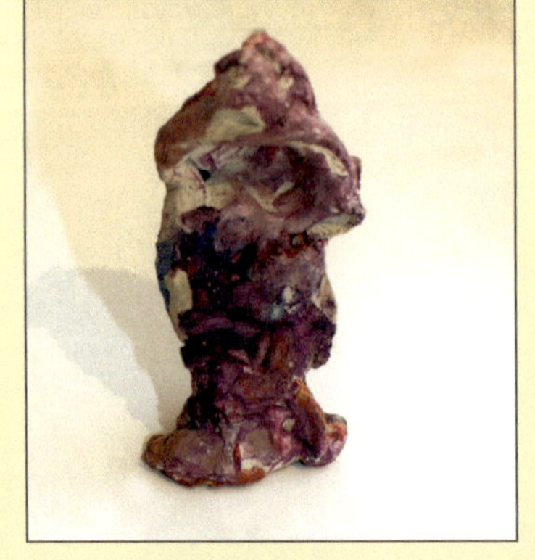

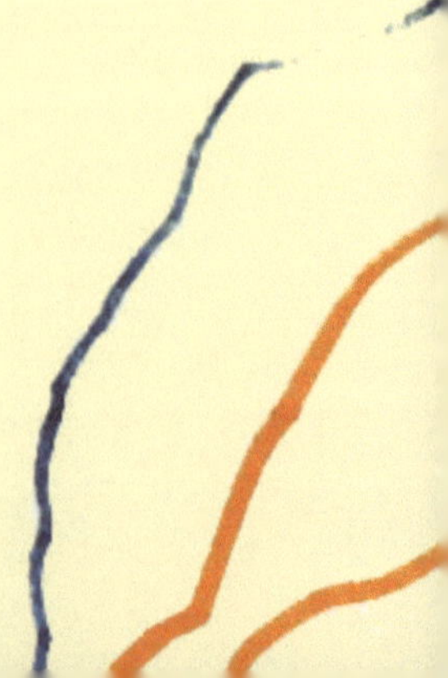

TALIA

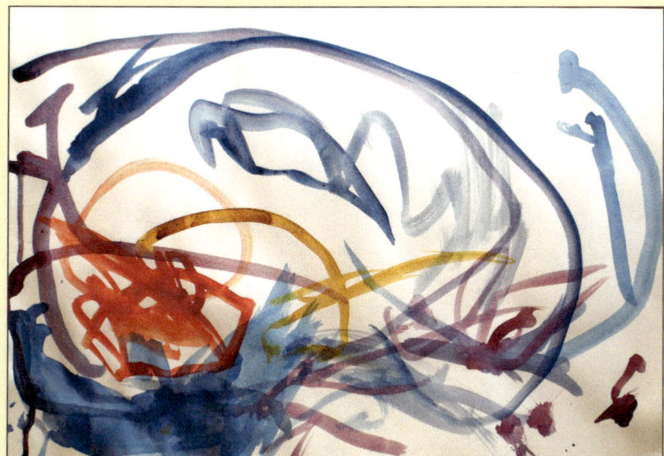

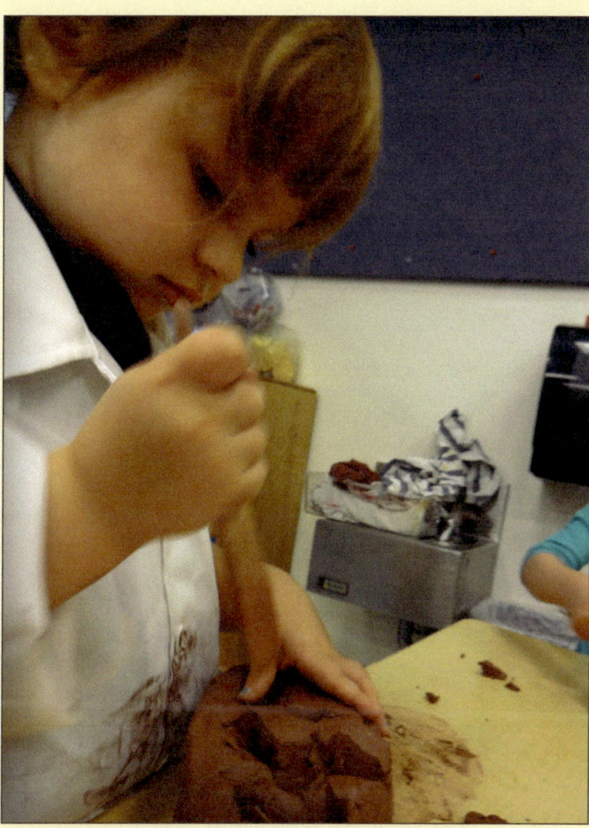

ABOUT THE ARTIST

Talia likes to share her artworks with her teachers and friends, and often brings over her paintings to ask, "What do you notice in my painting?" She enjoys painting, collage, and clay, and likes to work both in the art studio and in the classroom. Baby [Talia's doll] accompanies Talia in her artistic explorations, and is often asked by Talia to touch the clay or the glue as well.

Talia likes to experiment with various tools, routinely changing one for another: "I need a tool to break. Now I'm gonna use this tool. I wanna work with the sponge now."

IN HER OWN WORDS

I'm 4. I like to paint, I like to snuggle with my mommy. I like drawing with crayons with pink, purple, red, and blue! Baby's favorite color is yellow because she has a yellow dress! I like to play with my toys. Millions of toys!

I want this painting because I like this one because my favorite color is red and blue.

I like the blue and the purple. There's purple right there! Purple is also my favorite color.

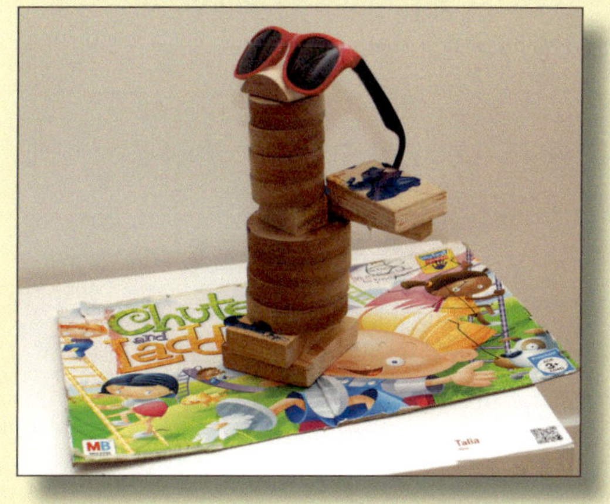

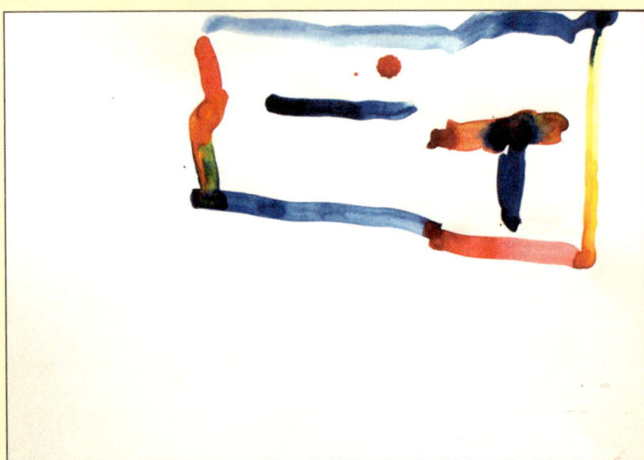

UMA

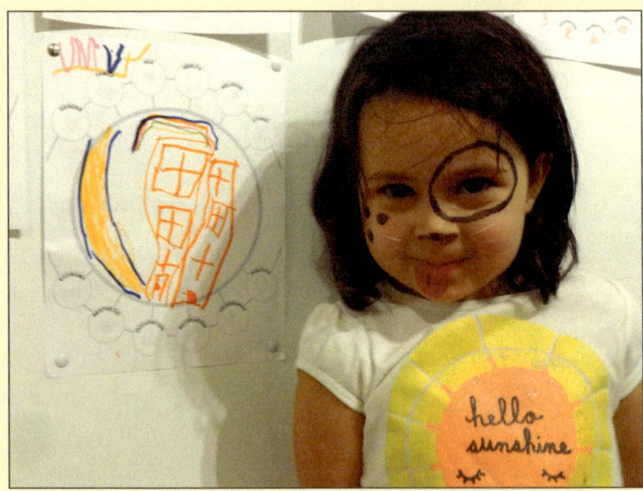

ABOUT THE ARTIST

Uma enjoys the peace of the art studio, especially when she gets to work on her own. Although she enjoys many different materials and techniques, she has a long-time passion for collage and beading, which she does with persistence and intensity. Uma's tenacity helps her find solutions for the things she needs fixed, like using pieces of clay to lock the edges of her beading wire. "I do this so the beads don't fall off. I got the idea from taping it [the clay]," Uma explains. Uma's love for animals is often present in her artmaking, and her dog Lola is both the inspiration for and the recipient of many drawings, paintings, and bead accessories such as necklaces, collars, or toys.

IN HER OWN WORDS

I like beading and collage. Collage on paper. I like the colors. My favorite color is pink. I like to mix colors to make pink. Red and white. I figured that out the first time I mixed them together. I like to look at art. It makes me feel happy.

You can't touch it. I made it out of clay and wire. I needed clay to put the wire in and I put beads on the wire. Only the ones with big holes fit. It's clay that we can paint. It does not have a name. It's a construction. I like that I can paint it.

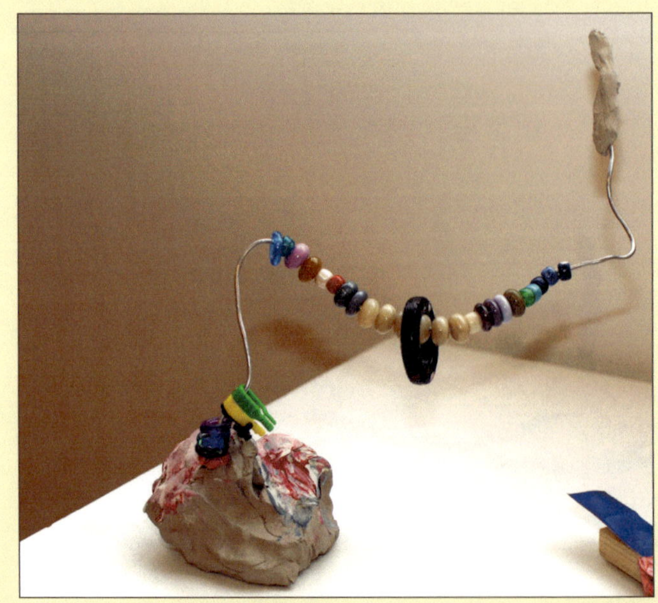

WILLIAM

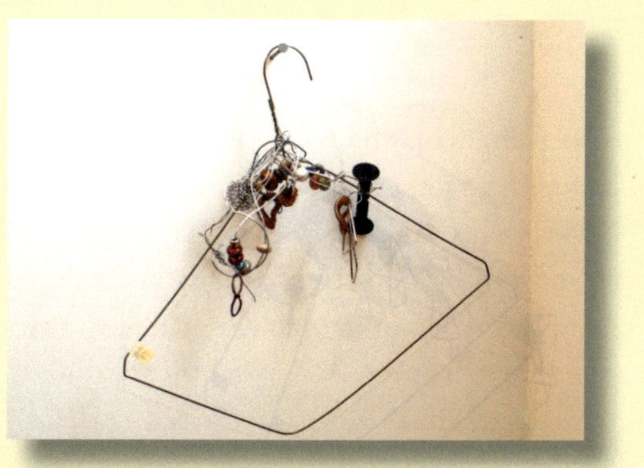

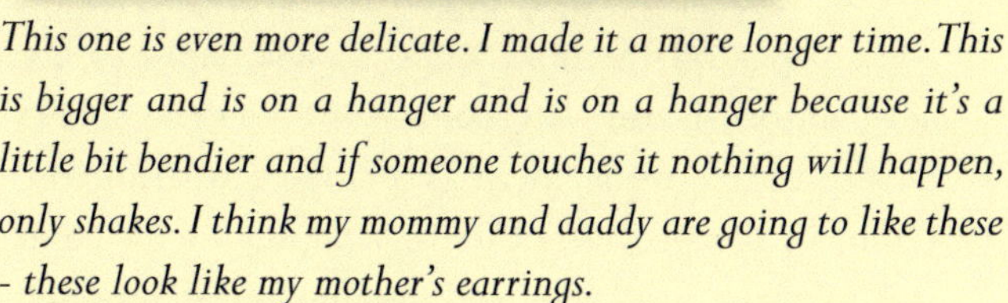

This one is even more delicate. I made it a more longer time. This is bigger and is on a hanger and is on a hanger because it's a little bit bendier and if someone touches it nothing will happen, only shakes. I think my mommy and daddy are going to like these - these look like my mother's earrings.

ABOUT THE ARTIST

In the art studio, William explores materials and tools with joy. Very attentive to his friends, he shares his expertise by providing explanations and ideas on how to use tools to change materials in specific ways — but not doing it for them. He often recalls prior explorations and brings that knowledge into whatever it is that he is working on, both in his narratives and with specific properties and possibilities of the materials. He is aware of the complexity of some of his projects, and embraces them with enthusiasm, as he did with his wire sculpture.

IN HIS OWN WORDS

See what I'm making? I think it's gonna take a preeeety long time. Mine is very delicate. It looks like your brain. It all giant scribble stuff so it looks like a brain.

Now I'm 5. I make beautiful stuff, everything I make is so beautiful, I like it. I like to make different kinds of art. I'm having fun with this one!

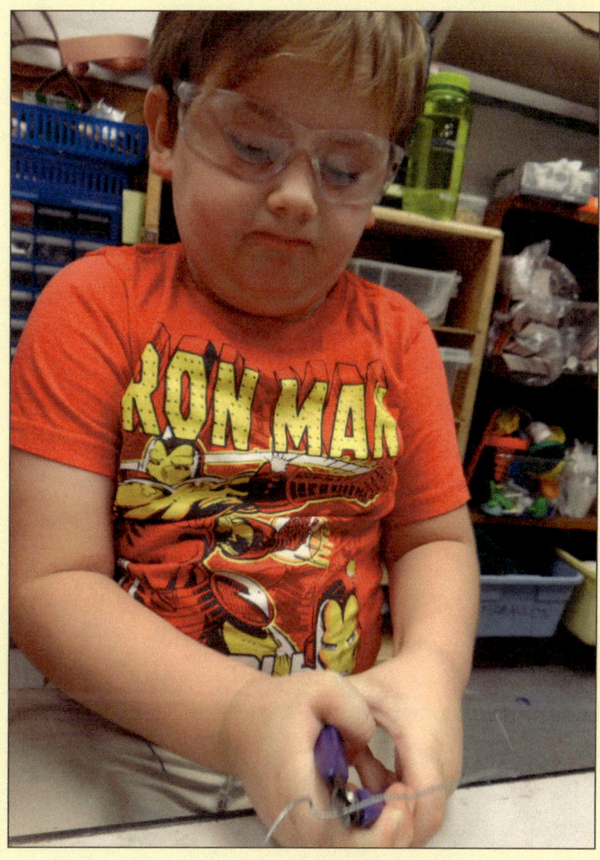

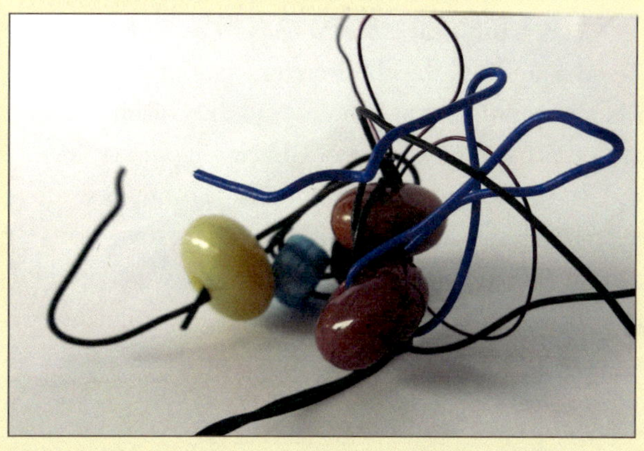

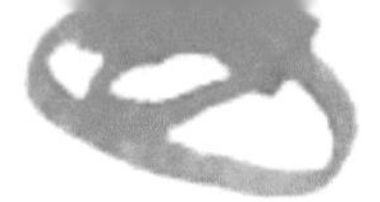

In every step of the show, toddlers and preschoolers are invited to be active participants and to make the exhibition their own. As the master-curator, it is my objective to create opportunities for children to see themselves as crucial participants and potentially feel a sense of ownership over the exhibition. The very young children in the infant room, however, have fewer opportunities to interact with the show in such an active manner, and finding ways to help them develop a similar sense of ownership over the exhibition presents a curatorial challenge. The infants' relationship with the materials is more in the process of exploration and less in the finished pieces, and they don't necessarily always recognize themselves in their paintings and other pieces.

One way of creating opportunities for that personal identification with the exhibition to happen, is to make integral in the exhibition certain objects that the babies have interacted with in the classroom as part of their experimentations with materials. That transference of materials in the classroom to becoming materials in the exhibition space has been a constant element in RGC shows.

For this year's *Broken Things Can Be Beautiful Things* exhibition, the children throughout the Center had been interested in boxes and 3D collages, and based on that interest, I started bringing boxes covered in watercolor paper to the infant room as well. We started by playing with the boxes as toys, using them in different ways. When the infants were familiar with the boxes, we linked this play to their experiences with watercolor paints, and children used the boxes to paint with and to paint on, exploring the two materials together in their own ways.

Noam, who at the time was very interested in cars and buses and often brought his yellow school bus toy to the painting table, decided to use the boxes as things that move, driving them around as he hummed car noises. Tulasi exercised her fine motor skills by carefully peeling much of the watercolor paper off the box, while Sahana chose to use her paintbrush and watercolor paints to make marks on the boxes, using them as a surface to paint on. Odin, in the process of getting familiar with paint as a material itself, enjoyed tapping and drumming on the boxes, while every now and then dipping his finger in the paints.

For the weeks following, the boxes remained in the classroom and the infants kept playing with them and making marks on them with crayons and other tools. So when the time came for the art exhibition and the boxes were positioned as a central part of the show, the infants had elements that they could more easily connect to, objects that they repeatedly interacted with in the classroom and that now in the gallery they could recognize as their own.

"Me!" Noam said as he walked up to the corner where the boxes were set out to be played with. "Me!" Callie called out as she pointed to the torn painting she chose to exhibit. "Me! Apple!" Liam shouted, as he ran towards his apple painting on the other end of the gallery, a painting that he worked on during his first weeks in the toddler room.

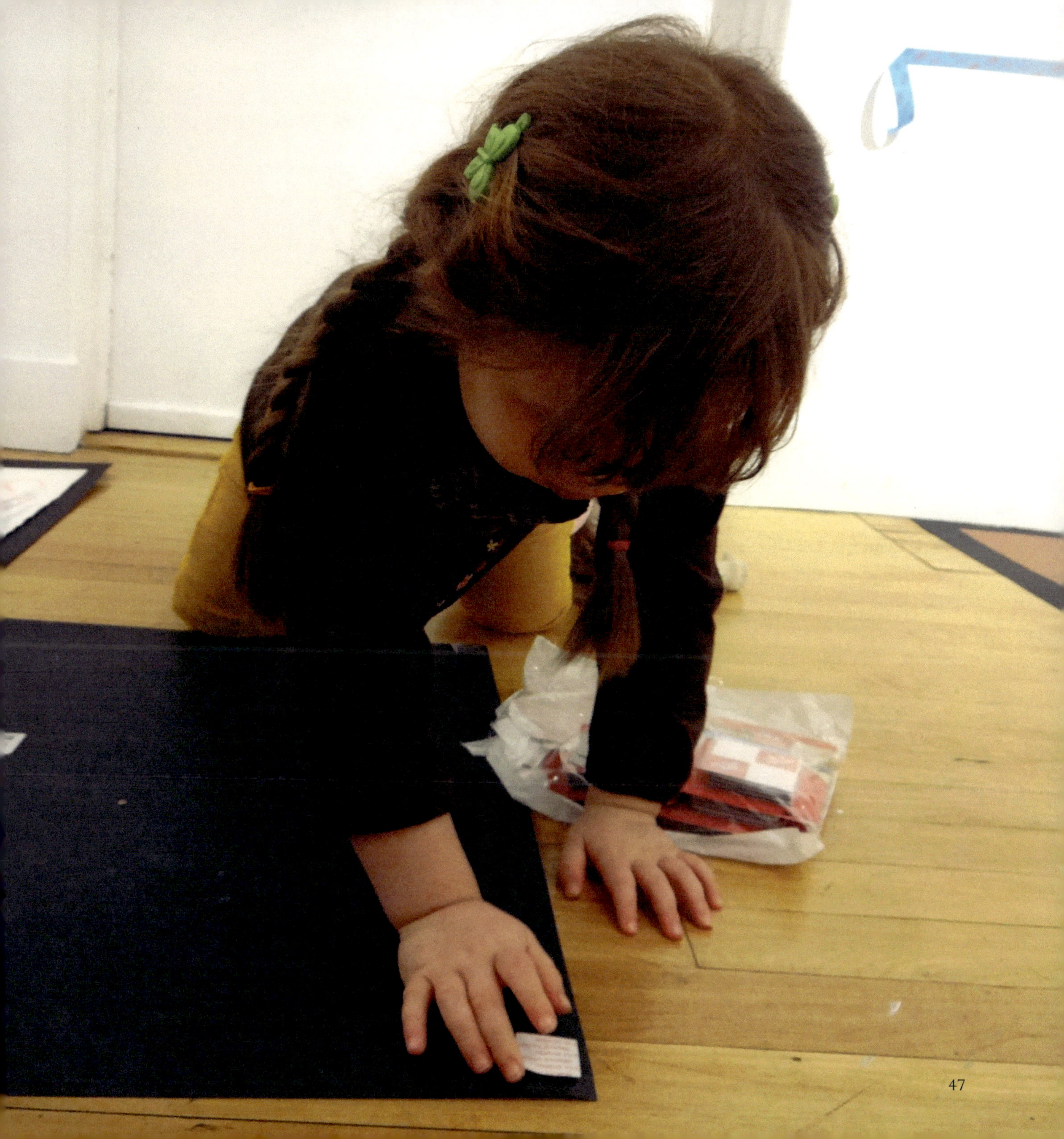

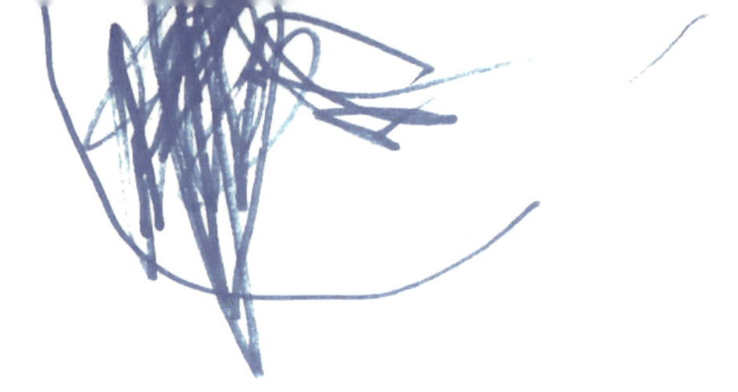

"I remember the pudding box!" Hari excitedly states as he shows his mother his "Tower" piece.

For several weeks, Hari was hard at work on his 3D tower collage, gluing boxes of different sizes and shapes together, painting them over, and decorating them with buttons and other small items. As the tower got taller and taller and eventually towered above him, the chocolate pudding box that he placed somewhere halfway in the construction remained his favorite, and he pointed it out every time he talked about his work. Lillian also worked on a box collage and finished it up with a joyful and messy sensory experience of paper maché, spreading stripes of gluey newsprint on her construction. Like Hari and Lilllian, many children this year enjoyed working with boxes - even baby Henry had a good time tapping on them, listening to the sounds they made.

All of this box experimentation came together again in the exhibition's reception. Boxes were a big part of the activities, aimed at bringing children, families, staff, friends, and visitors together in collaborative art-making. Using boxes that families and staff had helped to collect in the weeks preceding the reception, children and families worked on a community 3D collage. Nearby, more boxes of all sizes and shapes were made available in an interactive photo booth.

The photo booth was run by Callie's dad Jono, and on the night on the reception, children and adults enthusiastically played with boxes in various ways, opening their arms out to fly like Hiwa, looking through rolls to see what came up on the other side like Liam and Miguel, sailing in a boat-box like Sofia, or peeling off and unwrapping every last piece of paper as Paco did when he finally decided it was time for some unwrapping to happen.

Among the drawing, playing, flying boxes, and acting like superheroes, portraits and family portraits were taken, and many playful interactions happened. As children and families frolicked and enjoyed the setting, everyone's hard work in wrapping box after box paid off. Between moments of box constructing and deconstructing, collaging and creating, playing and drawing, and enjoying and consuming the large cake that was baked by one of the teachers and decorated by children and parents, the art show became everyone's art show.

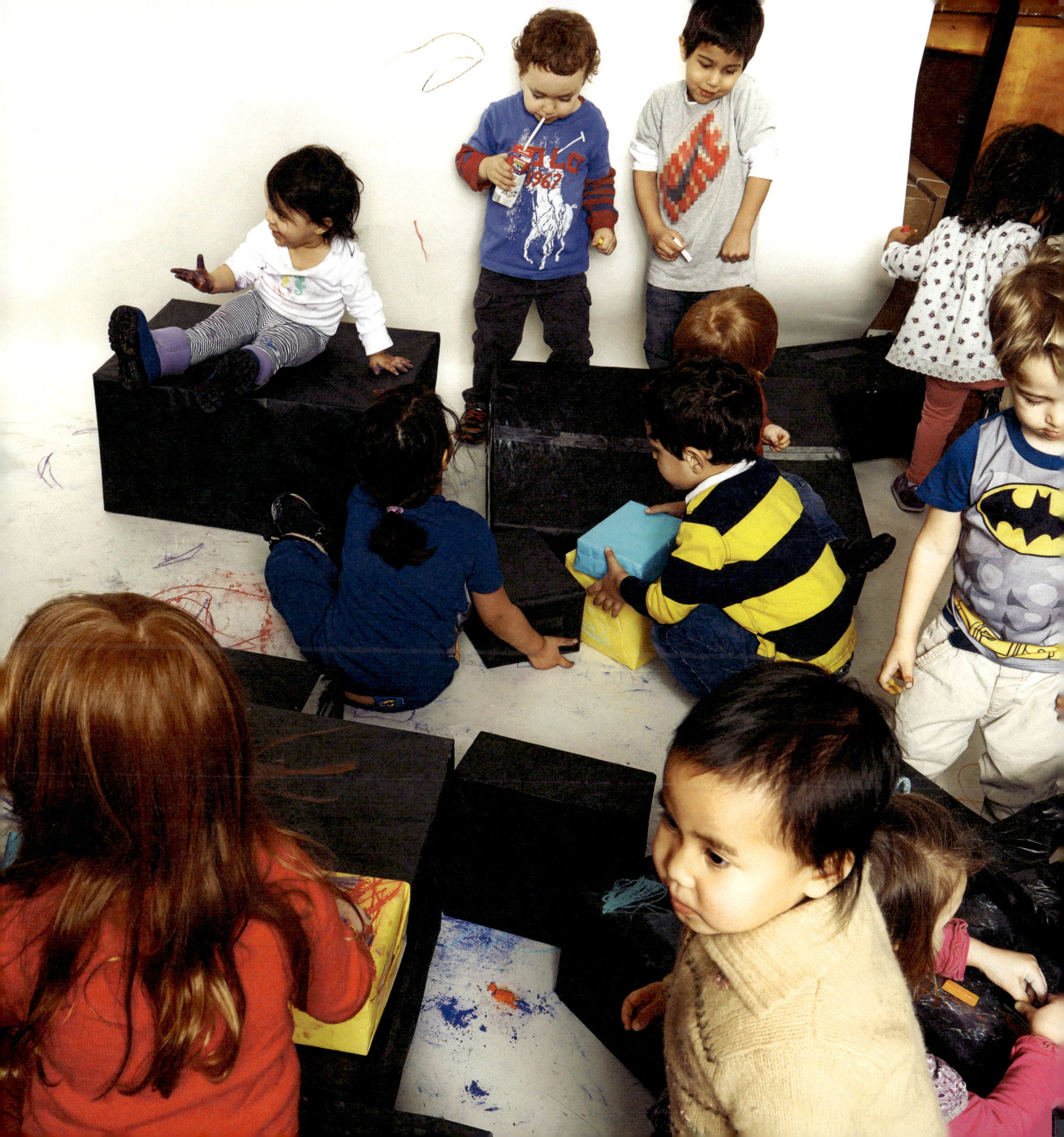

CONCLUSION

Our last meeting with the preschooolers about the art exhibition is filled with excitement, as we share our thoughts. "My art show is really pretty," Dylan starts, while Talia tells us how much she liked having her paintings up in the gallery. But "[taking down the artwork] makes me sad," Paco interjects. "I really wanna keep it up. Because I love doing art!" Carter adds. William, Leah, and Haram, despite how excited and engaged they have been in the exhibition, are happy about taking their artwork home to their parents - as other children are too. Annabelle, on the other hand, sees the bright side of both situations: "I'm happy either way because when they're up and we can see them beautiful in a show, and when they're down we can take them home. That's why I'm happy either way."

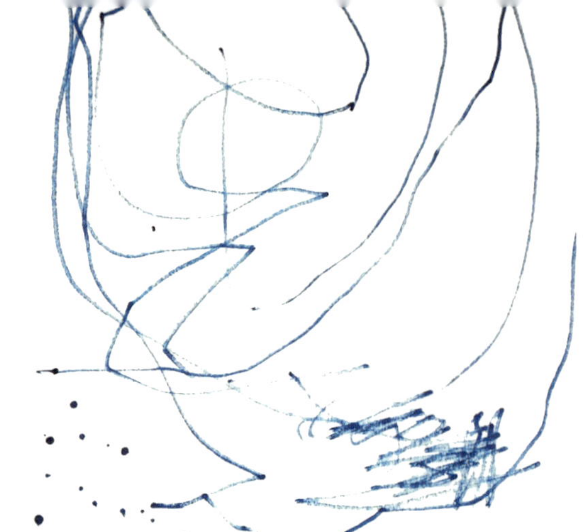

Like Annabelle, I also miss our art exhibition. There is something very special about walking into Macy Gallery every morning to be greeted by my children's work. As I take my daily walk by the gallery, I am reminded of special moments of our experiences together, and of how this exhibition is an effort of many hands, hearts, and minds. I think back to Liam's first morning in the art studio, working on the floor by the door until he felt safe enough to go in, and of how he now deeply engages with art both in the studio and in Macy Gallery so much so that he responds with a resounding "no" every time I ask if he is ready to go back to the classroom.

I think back to then-toddler Sofia's breathtaking discovery of how red and blue mix together in her hands to create purple, and how she was so excited to share that with everyone around her. I think back to the many moments Seungha took to closely observing her peers using their paints, and how she brought all that gained expertise to practice when she decided she was ready to touch the paints herself.

But a part of me - maybe also like Annabelle - is okay with letting go. It is now time to give other artists and curators their turn in the gallery, and that is also an important thing to learn. And we get to take our art home with us. As for me, I have an incredible amount of joyful, inspiring, and powerful memories to live with - as I hope our children do as well.

As the children and I gave the show one last look, we came together as a group to read the comments visitors left in our guest book. It is always an exciting moment to consider our audience and most children are happy to find a note from a loved one, someone's parent, or maybe a person they showed around in a guided tour. Many comments mentioned specific elements of artworks, like colors or types of lines, and the children looked around to identify them. As we read comments from previous years, the preschoolers enjoyed talking about their time as infants and toddlers, and some of them recalled the previous year's exhibition.

As we recalled how we installed the exhibition, we talked about how to now de-install it: we needed to take the pieces down from the wall and pedestals and peel off the mounting squares with which we hung the work up. In small groups, children went up to the gallery to take their work off the walls and bring it back to their classrooms.

Toddlers and preschoolers helped with the works of their younger siblings and other infants, and soon the gallery walls were bare again. Participating in this process can be important for children's understanding and interpreting of the temporary nature of an art exhibition such as ours. As much as they are used to visiting different exhibitions in the gallery, ours is a special one, and to see everything suddenly gone can be confusing.

Pointing at the spots on the wall where Clara's and his own collage used to be, Miguel asked, "Where's Clara's? Where's mine?" in his first visit to the gallery after the exhibition's close. He eventually did take his artwork down back to the toddler room himself - but in some way, it's still hard to believe it's not up in the gallery anymore.

Now that the exhibition has been de-installed, it is time to hang up the community artwork that was created during the reception, and that will stay at the RGC. As I walk through our hallway, where year after year, art show after art show, another community piece finds its place, I am reminded of how lucky I am to share my days with such wonderful children and fellow teachers, in such a supportive and safe environment, covered in paint, clay, and glue. And, I can't wait for next year's art show.

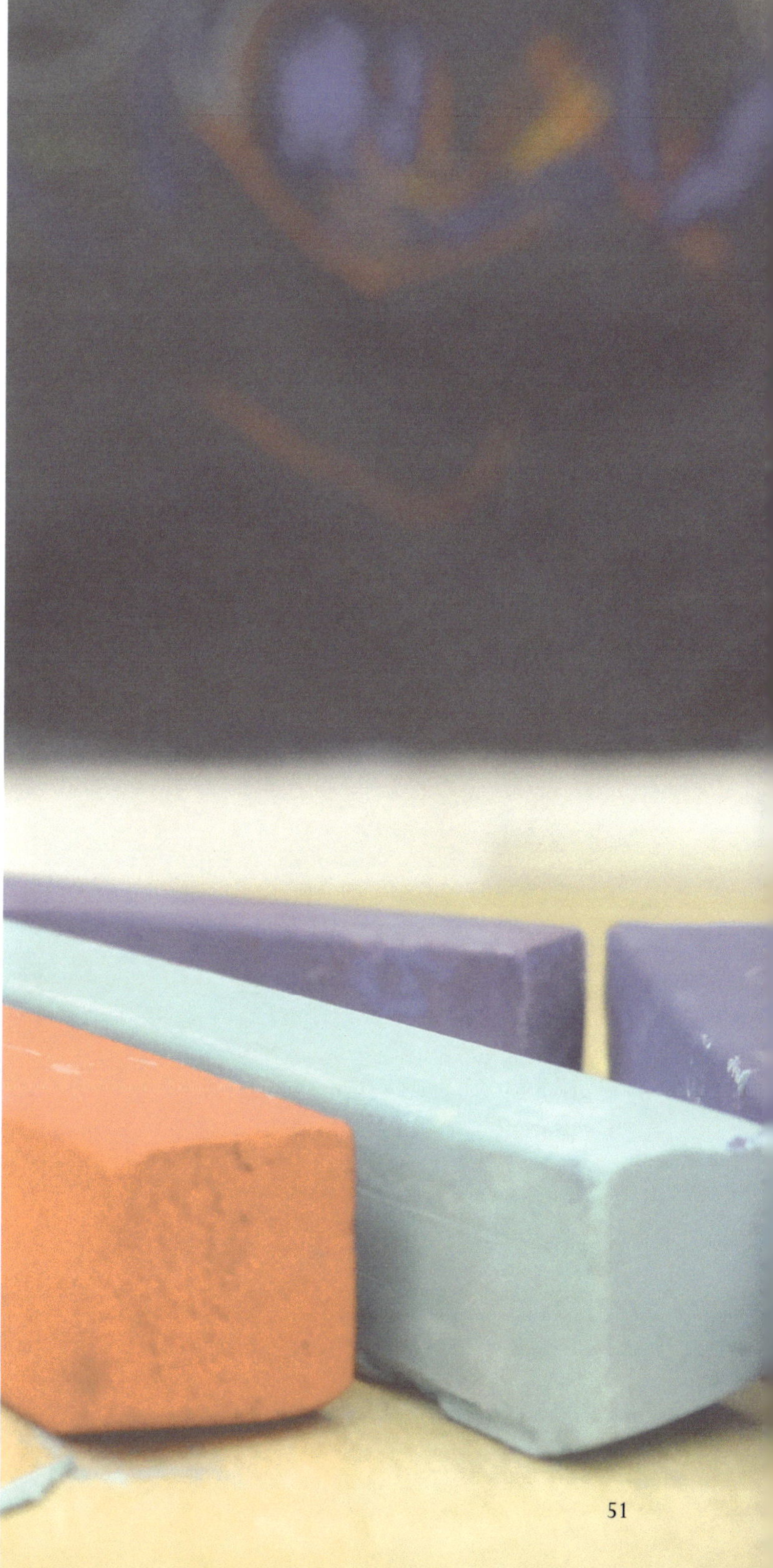

OLD & NEW FRIENDS

Sammie, Luka, Derrick, Colten, Luca, and Wynter were also with us for a portion of our artistic explorations during the creation of this book. We enjoyed their company, and look forward to many more explorations together!

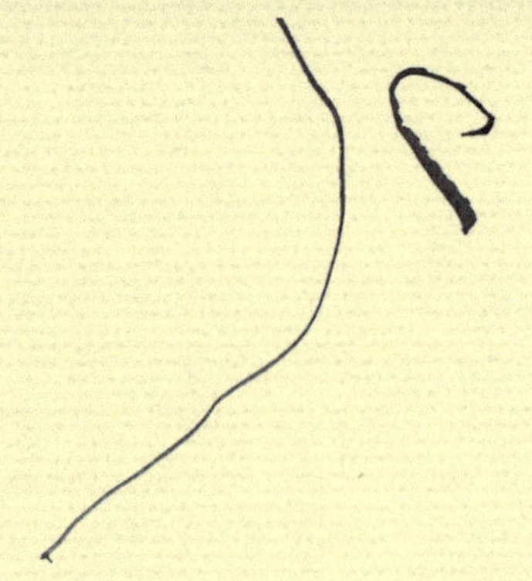

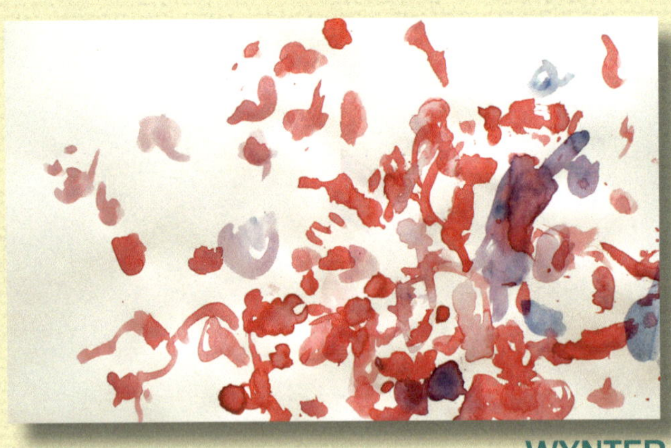

WYNTER

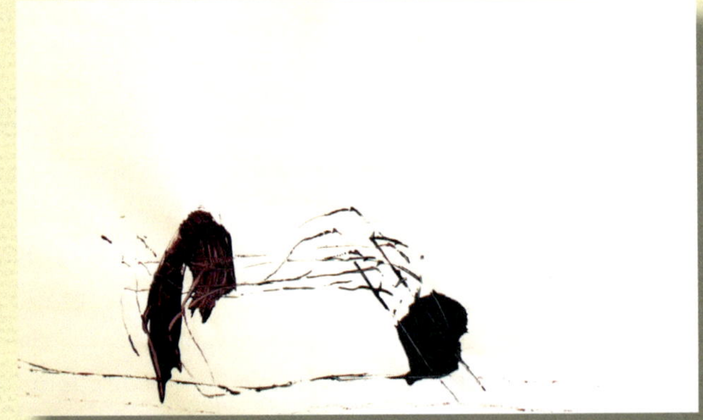

COLTEN

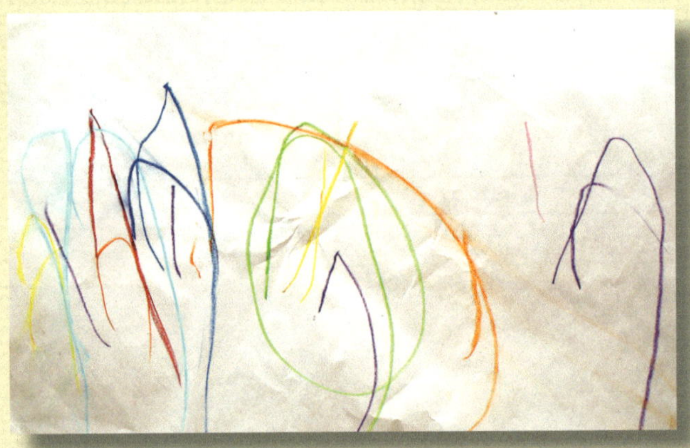

SAMMIE

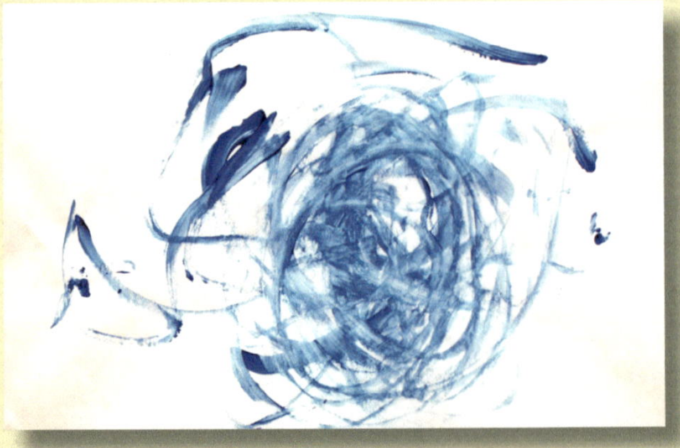

LUKA

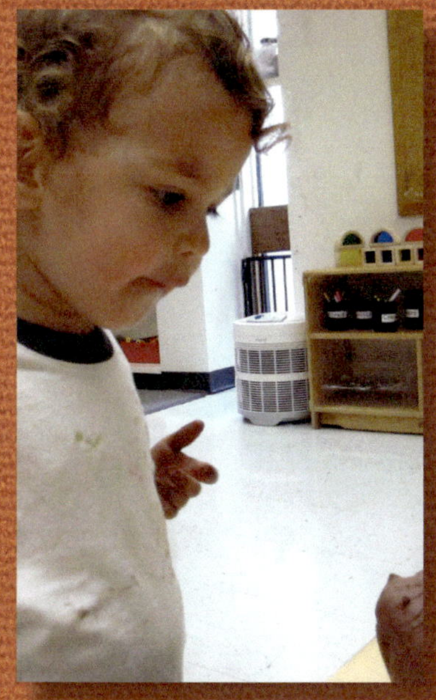

SAMMIE

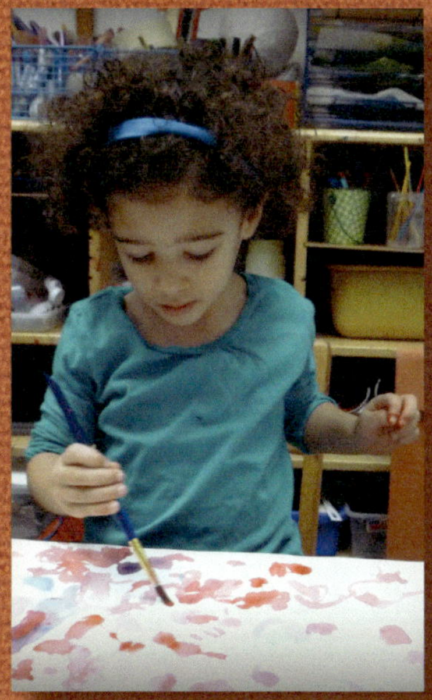

WYNTER

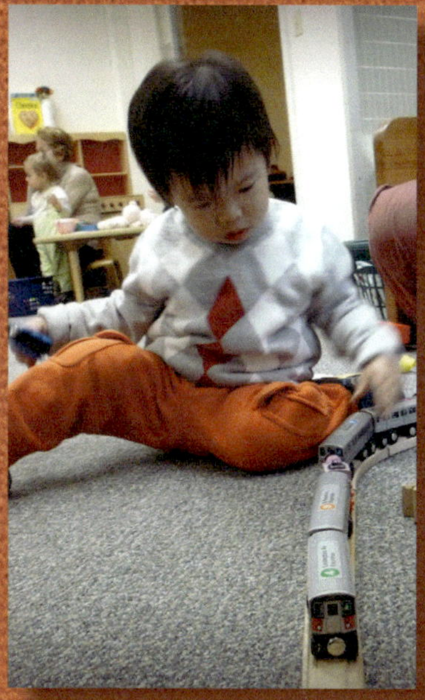

DERRICK

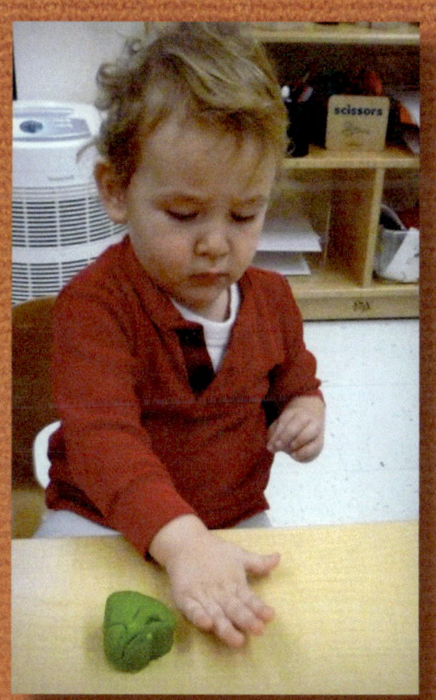

LUCA

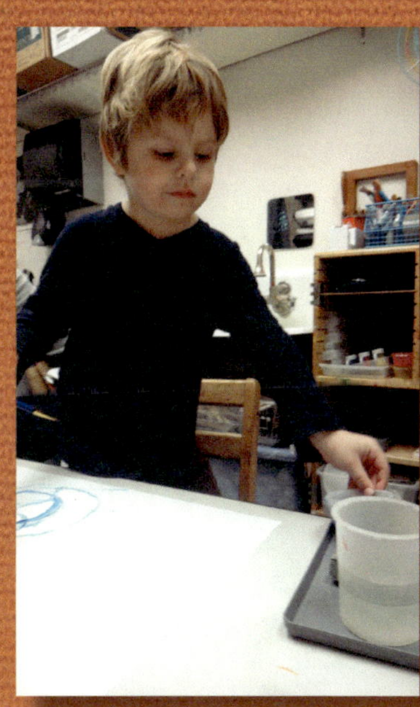

LUKA

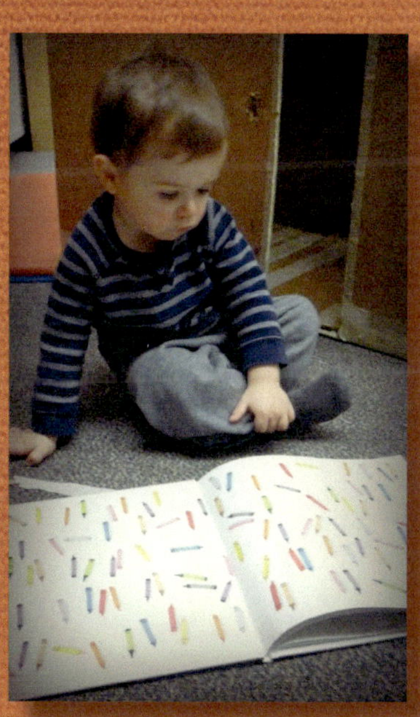

COLTEN

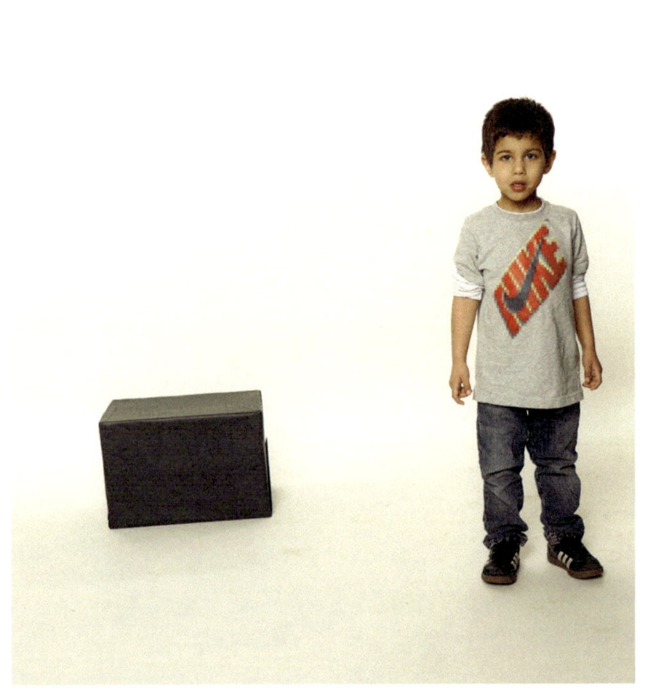
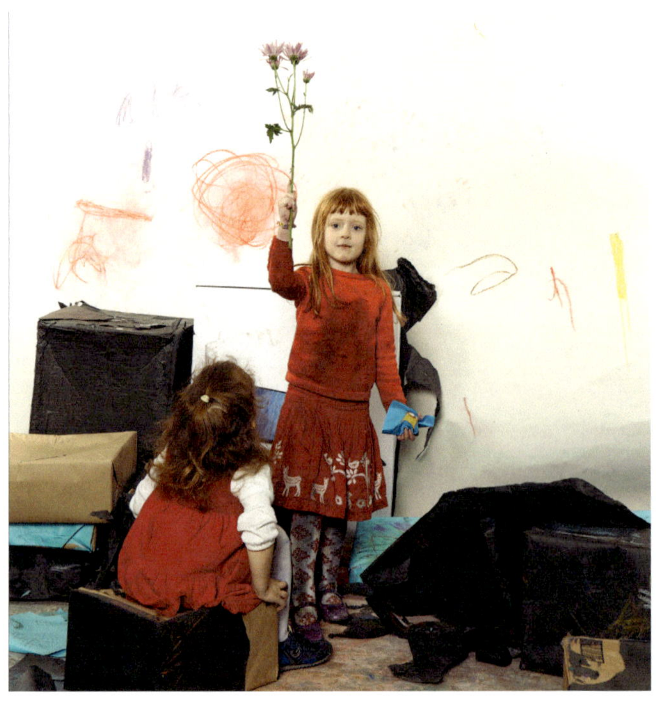

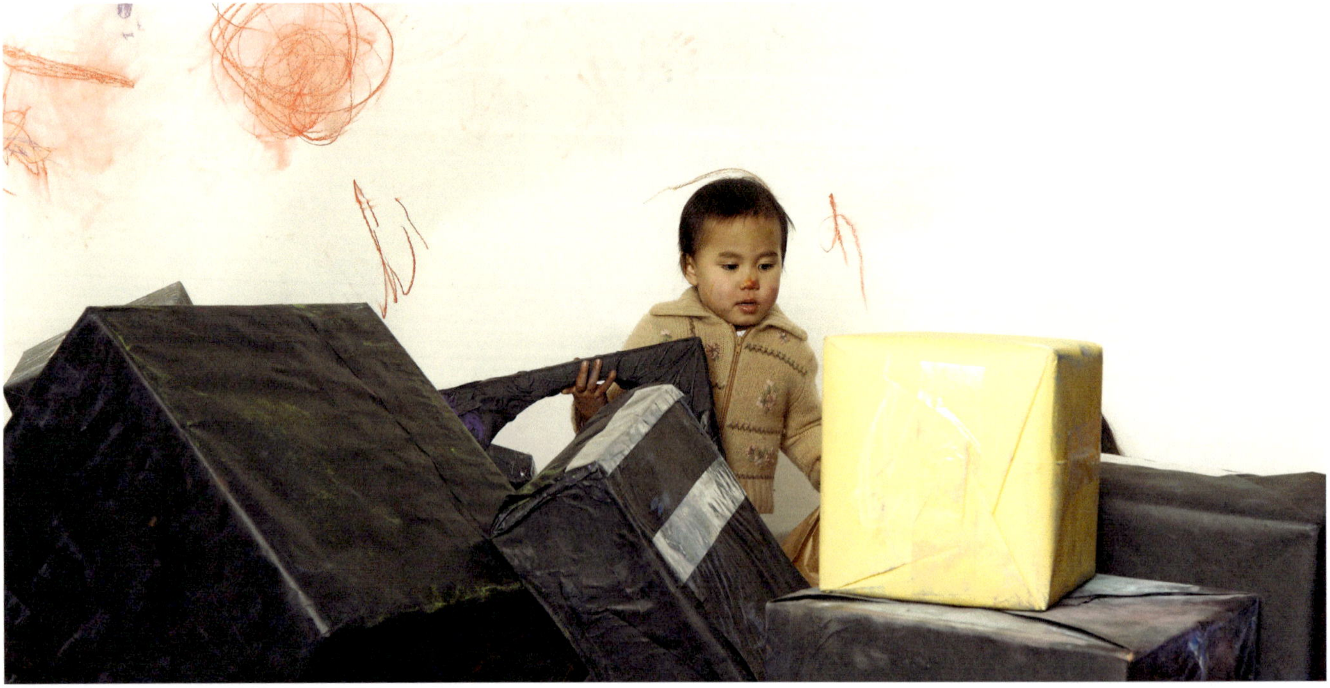

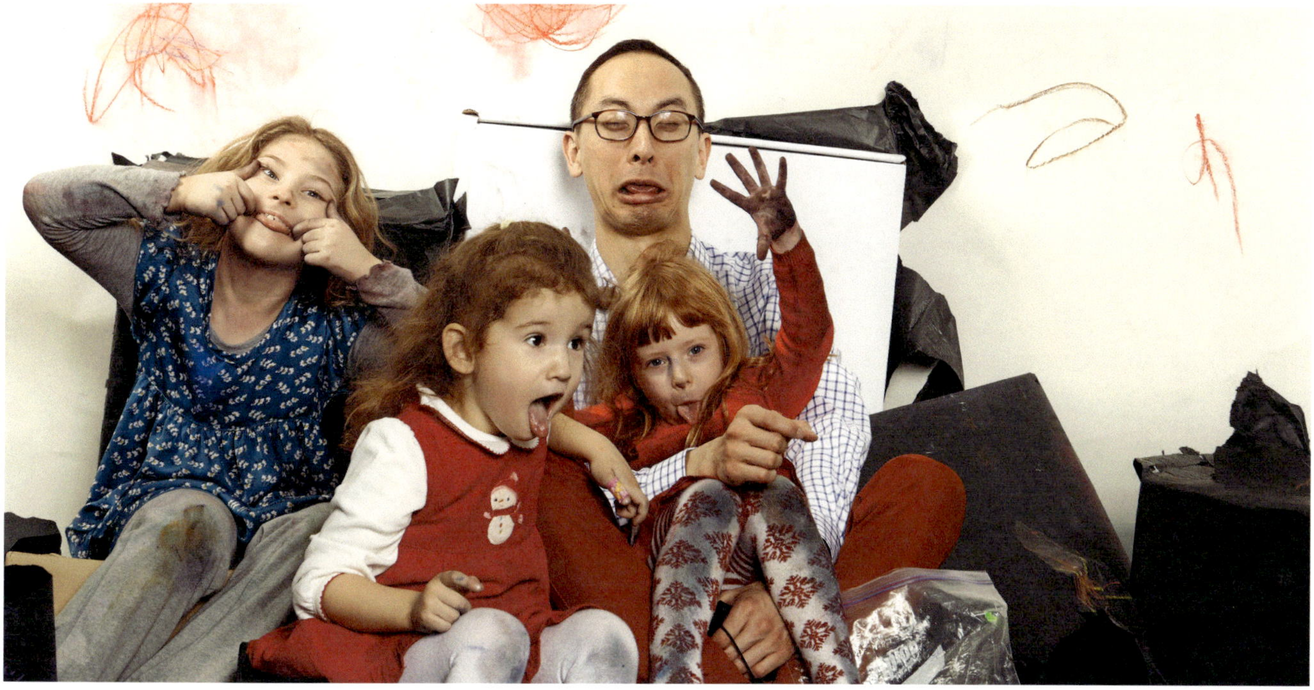

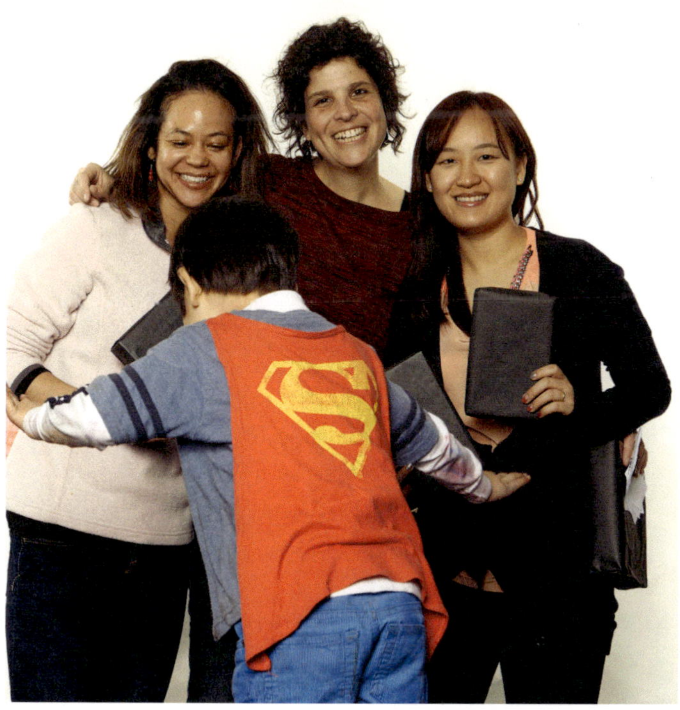

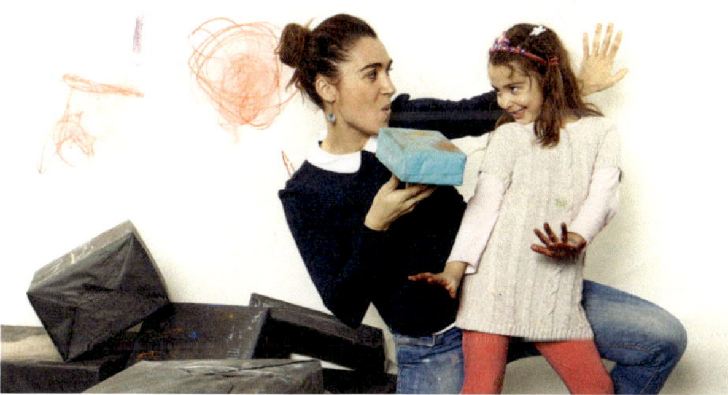

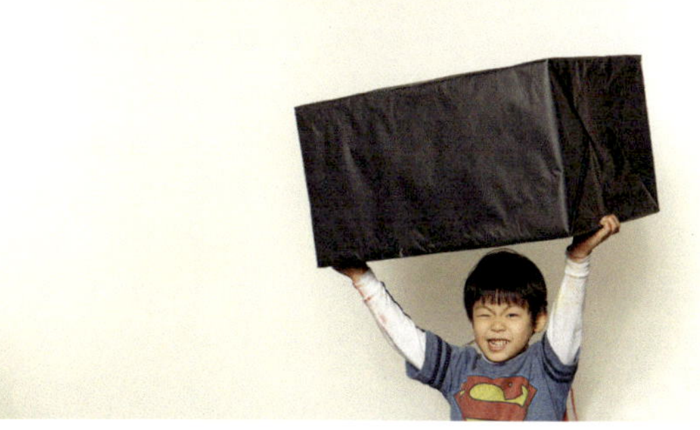

INDEX

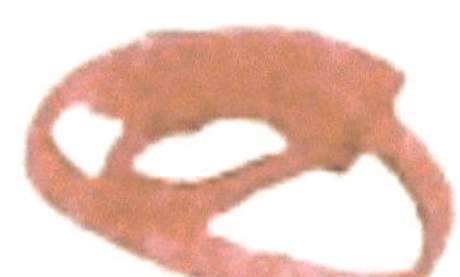

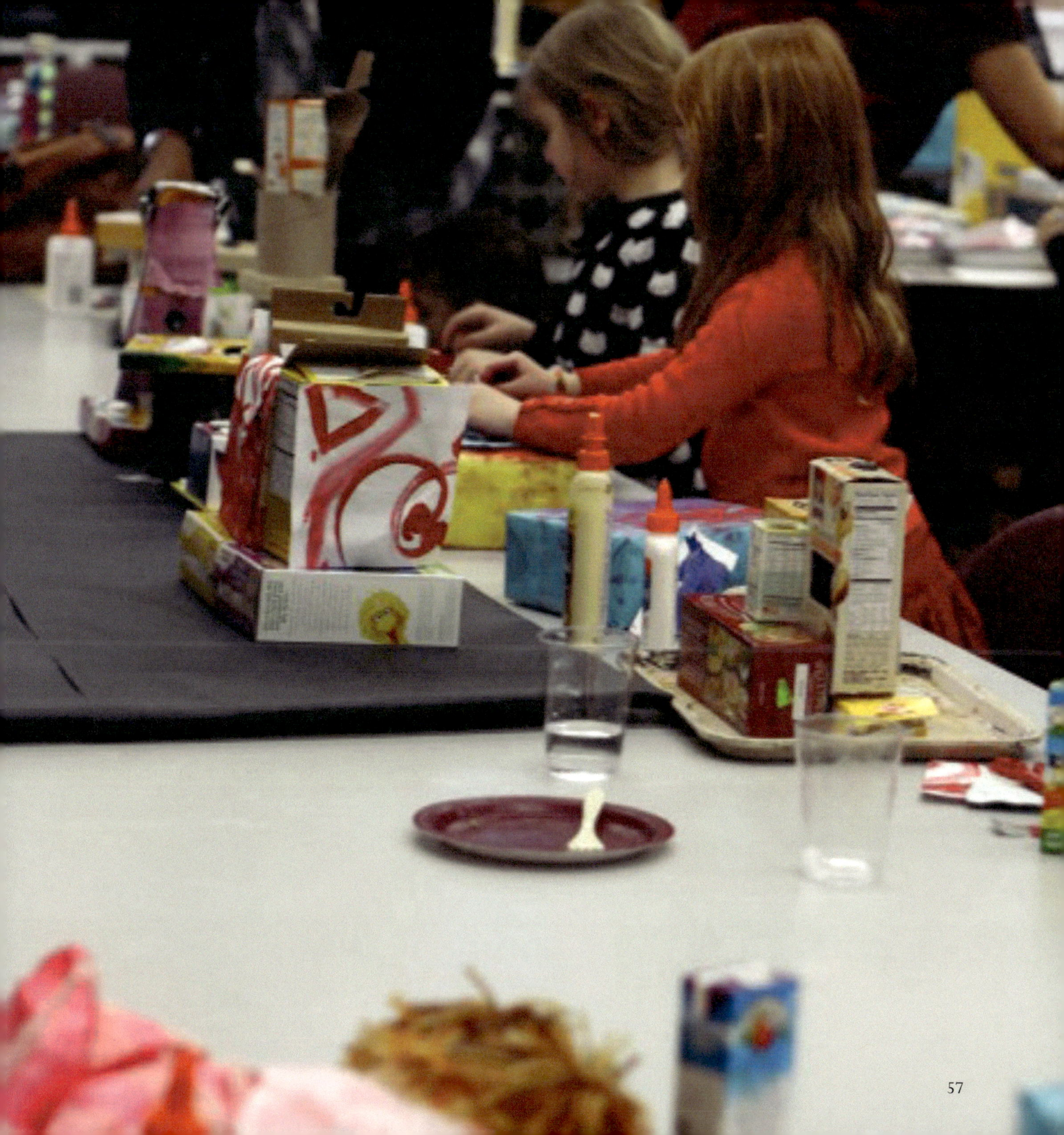

Made in the USA
Monee, IL
06 March 2026